BY THE SAME AUTHOR:

ABC of Alpha and Beta
Battle of White Plains
Bear Market Characteristics
Bias in Daily and Weekly Wave Patterns
Chess Openings Simplified
Circumpolar Constellations
Filtered Waves Basic Theory
Fitting Linear and Curvilinear Regression
    Lines with a Pocket Calculator
How Do You Use the Slide Rule
Log Scale Construction
Manipulating Indicators with a Micro
Market Indicators and Growth Company Ratings
M and W Wave Patterns

BEHAVIOR OF PRICES ON WALL STREET

BY ARTHUR A. MERRILL

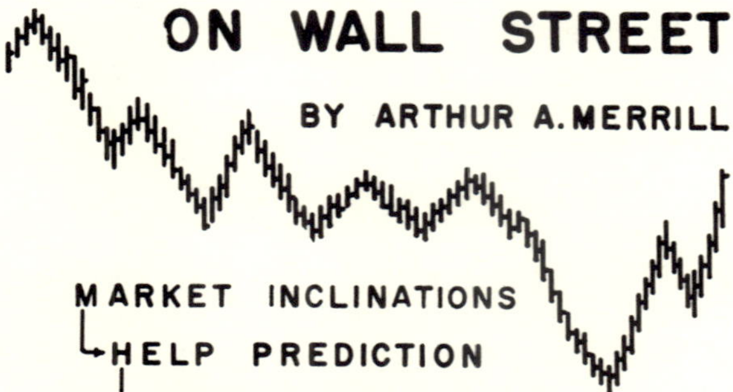

MARKET INCLINATIONS
→HELP PREDICTION
→PRODUCE PROFITS

SECOND EDITION - REVISED

Published by

The Analysis Press, Chappaqua, New York

Second Edition Revised

Printed in the United States of America
Published by
The Analysis Press, Chappaqua, New York
10 9 8 7 6 5 4 3 2

Library of Congress Cataloging in Publication Data
Merrill, Arthur A.
Behavior of Prices on Wall Street
Includes Bibliographies
1. Wall Street 2. Stock Exchange 3. Speculation
I. Title
Library of Congress Catalog Card No. 84-72279
ISBN 0-911894-49-7

DEDICATION:

To ELSIE

Always helpful; always inspiring.

"I often say that when you can measure what you are speaking about, and express it in numbers, you know something about it; but when you cannot express it in numbers, your knowledge is of a meagre and unsatisfactory kind; it may be the beginning of knowledge, but you have scarcely in your thoughts advanced to the stage of Science, whatever the matter may be."

Sir William Thomson, Lord Kelvin

INDEX:

APPENDIXES:

IN APPRECIATION

The suggestions made by the following have been especially helpful: Ralph J. Acampora, A. Hamilton Bolton, Donna Breed, Robert W. Breiling, Dr.Edward R. Dewey, William S. Doane, Dr.Jack A. Dorland, Dernell Every, James Fraser, Norman G. Fosback, Devin A.Garrity, Floyd L. Hogan, Christopher R. Landmann, Harry W. Laubscher, S. Jay Levy, Maxine Lewis, Bernard L. Mazel, John R. McGinley Jr., Dr. William D. Merrill, Francis N. Millett, Robert R. Prechter, Richard Russell, George Seager, Gertrude Shirk, William P.Short, George E.Tener, and David Upshaw.

FOREWORD:

Wall Street has always been awash in available information. Much of that information can be useful at times, but very little of it is considered useful all of the time. For more than twenty-five years I have found the information available in "Behavior of Prices on Wall Street" useful all of the time. The dogeared condition of my personal copy bears mute testimony to the use I give it in dealing with the many questions about market action that come my way every day. It demonstrates the tendency for the stock market to rise at certain definite times, as well as its predilection for exhibiting weakness at other definite times. In underscoring the fact that the market does not move randomly, it provides information that has proven of use to investors and speculators alike.

As the author points out, this is a picture book where a chart can reveal countless statistics. I like to think of it as a travelogue through market time, where the journey has potential for substantially enlarging one's knowledge about the history of the stock market. Followers of Dow's Theory and Elliott's Theory will find data pertinent to their researches, while those who track the impact of Federal Reserve Board actions on the stock market will discover much to interest them. Much of this data will help to sweep away erroneous and misleading myths about market behavior that actually have little or no basis in fact but which have become accepted as fact over the years. There are no suppositions made and where any bias is indicated, it is the bias of the market itself for doing certain things at certain times. In a world where there is almost too much information at hand, this continues to be a valuable source book.

Harry W. Laubscher

1. AIM OF THIS BOOK:

There are inclinations or leanings in the behavior of the market. At certain predictable times it has a bias in the bullish direction; at other predictable times it has a downward bias.

A knowledge of these inclinations is useful in the timing of purchase or sale of stock.

A stock market bias results in a probability, not a certainty. For this reason, bias is not obvious. This book reports inclinations revealed by the simple but laborious act of consulting the record.

Most of the reports are simple counting; no mathematical knowledge is required. A few statistical significance tests are mentioned, but I've tried to translate the jargon into English. I promise not to mention heteroscedasticity.

This is essentially a picture book. Don't be misled by the brevity of the text; the charts summarize many thousands of observations.

The first edition of this book was published in 1966. It has been out of print for several years, although the Japanese translation is still available in Japan. When second hand copies of the first edition began to sell for five times the original list price, a new edition seemed to be a good idea.

This second edition is not a reprint. Charts and data have been brought up to date, and most of the text has been rewritten. New material has been added.

The original conclusions, however, haven't been changed. The new data supported and verified the original findings.

2.HOW SIGNIFICANT ARE THE CONCLUSIONS?

If, in the past, the records show that the market behavior exhibited more rises than declines at a certain time, could it have been by chance? Yes. If a medication produced cures more often than average, could it have been luck? Yes.

If so, how meaningful is the record?

Statisticians set up "confidence levels" to be helpful. If the result could have occurred by chance once in twenty repetitions of the record, you can have 95% confidence that the result isn't just luck. This level has been called "probably significant."

If the result could be expected by chance once in a hundred repetitions, you can have 99% confidence; this level has been called "significant."

If the expectation is once in a thousand repetitions, you can have 99.9% confidence that the result wasn't just a lucky record. This level has been called "highly significant."

These three levels are sometimes indicated on the charts in this book by the letters "PS", "S" or "HS".

For example, in Chapter 5, it's noted that the first day of the month was a rising day in 60.5% of the months from 1897 through 1983. A statistical test shows that this ratio could be expected only once in thousands of repetitions of the test period.

Perhaps this could be clarified by a parallel. Suppose that to test the accuracy of a roulette wheel, you spun it 1044 times, and 60.5% of the time the result was red and 39.5% black (assume a strange wheel with no 00!) You would have to repeat this lengthy experiment thousands of times to expect such a high ratio by chance; the wheel should be sent back to the shop for repair.

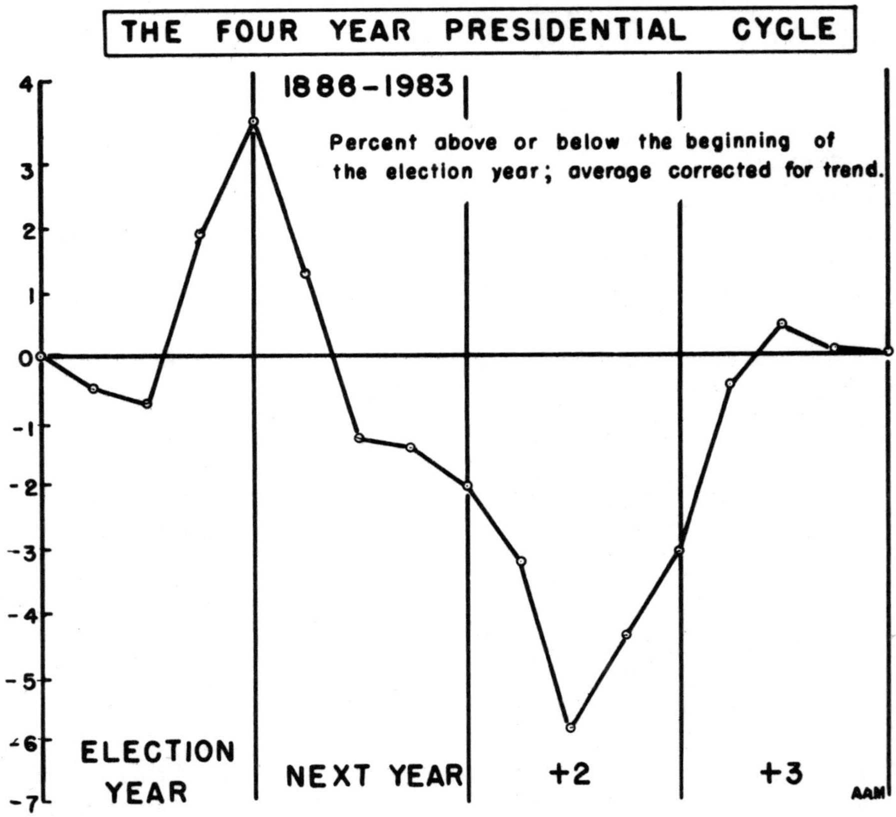
THE FOUR YEAR PRESIDENTIAL CYCLE
1886-1983
Percent above or below the beginning of the election year; average corrected for trend.
4
3
2
1
0
-1
-2
-3
-4
-5
-6
-7
ELECTION YEAR
NEXT YEAR
+2
+3
AAM

FIG.3.1

3. BEHAVIOR IN THE PRESIDENTIAL CYCLE

We have reviewed the behavior of the market through 24 presidential terms. There was extreme variation, and prices moved differently in each term. The averages, though, showed some interesting tendencies.

In Fig.3.1 the term is divided into sixteen three month periods, and the average change noted in each period.

Through the years, prices tended to rise more than they declined. This trend had to be corrected to make the cycle end at the level of its starting point.

Note the election year. Prices tended to droop in the first six months, but zoomed up in the second half.

After the election, prices averaged downward for a year and a half, reaching bottom in the middle of the second year after the election.

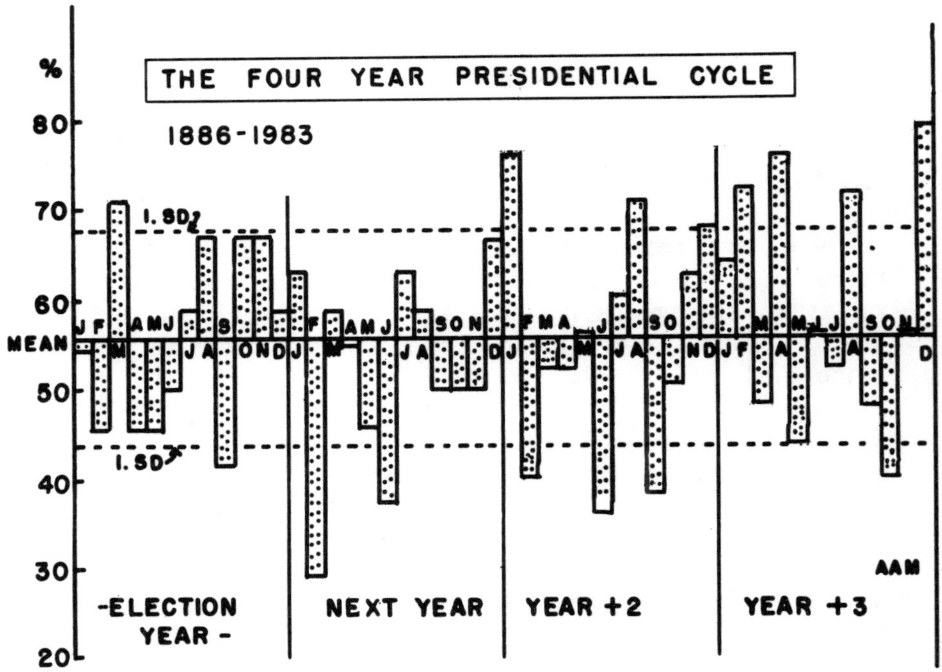

Example: In January, second year after election, prices rose in 19 years and declined in 6. years ; 19. is 76% of 25.

FIG.3.2

In Fig.3.2 the score was tabulated for each month of the term. The number of rises and declines were noted for each month, and the chart shows the percent of the time that the market rose in each month.

The bars are centered on the mean percentage of 56%. It's above 50% since there were were more rising months than declining months. The dashed lines marked "SD" are one standard deviation above and below the mean.

There are some interesting scores. Note that October and November in the election year have good scores, but December is close to average. Prices started to dive, on the average, in the following February.

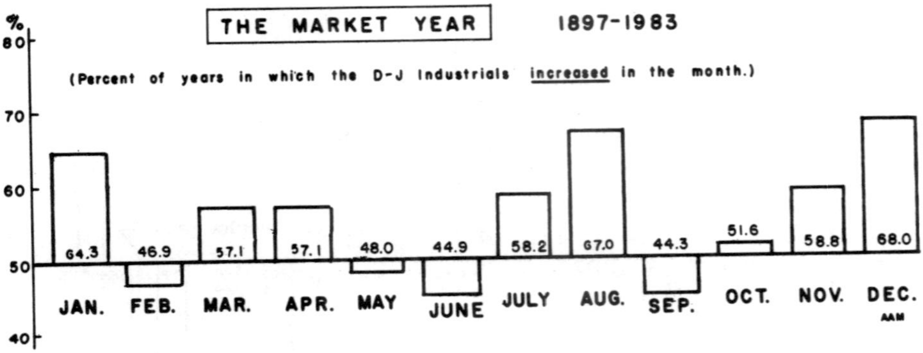

FIG.4.1

4. BEHAVIOR THROUGH THE YEAR

Fig 4.1 summarizes the monthly tendency of the market from 1886 through 1983.

The month with the best score is December. In this month the market rose in 66 of the 97 years, or 68.0% of the time.

Close behind December is the summer rally month of August. January followed in third place. The most bearish months are June and September.

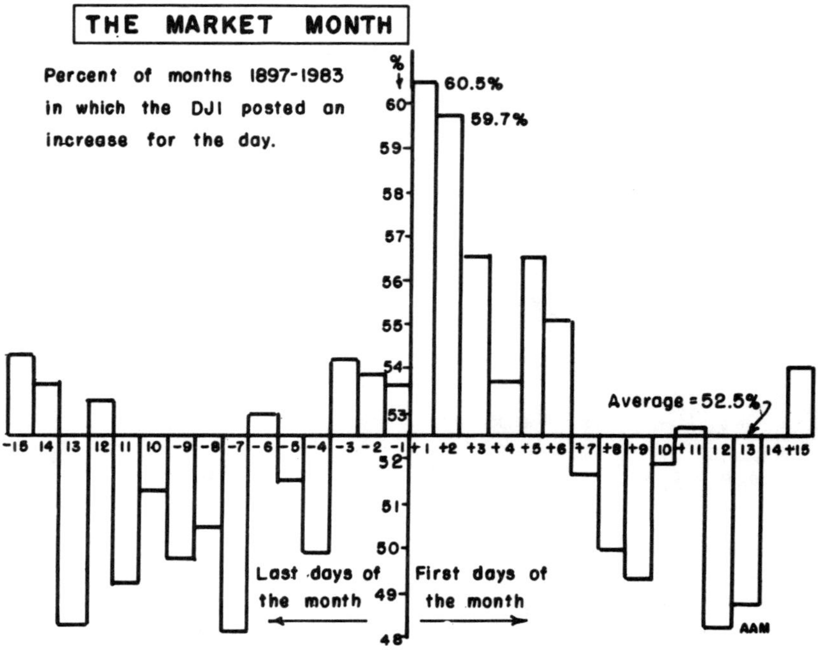

FIG.5.1

5. BEHAVIOR THROUGH THE MONTH

Fig.5.1 has been split in the middle. Because of the important beginning-of-the-month behavior, the first of the month has been placed in the middle of the chart.

The conclusion is clear; there is a definite bullish bias in the first week of the month. The bias is highly significant in the first two days of the month.

The second and third weeks have poor records. The end of the last week shows some improvement.

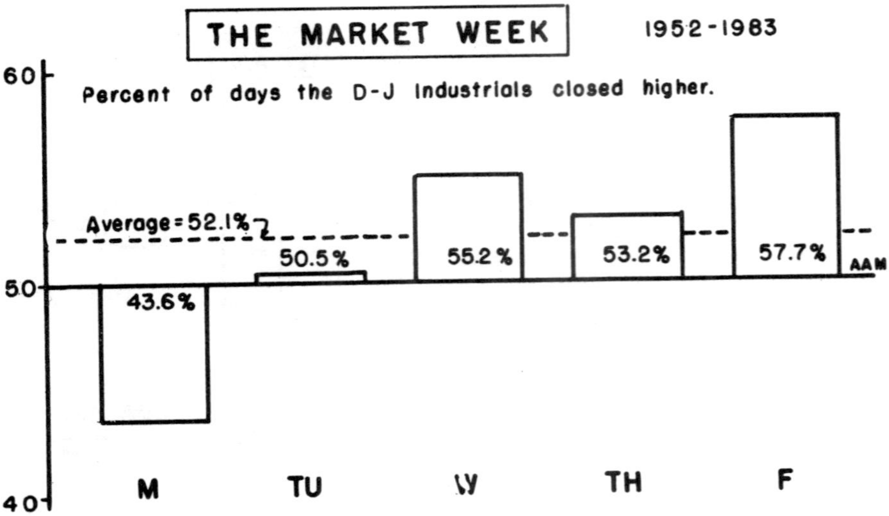

FIG.6.1

6. BEHAVIOR THROUGH THE WEEK

Before 1952, the market was open on Saturdays. Since that time we have had a five day week with a performance record summarized in Fig.6.1 .

Monday is truly a blue day. The market rose only 43.6% of the time, which is a highly significant deviation from average.

Friday, on the other hand is highly significant in the bullish direction. This is contrary to the lore of the market, since Friday is supposed to be a day when traders unload to free their minds for the weekend.

THE MARKET DAY

– Percent of trading days Jan. 1962 through Dec. 1974 in which the D-J industrials posted an increase from the preceding hour. –

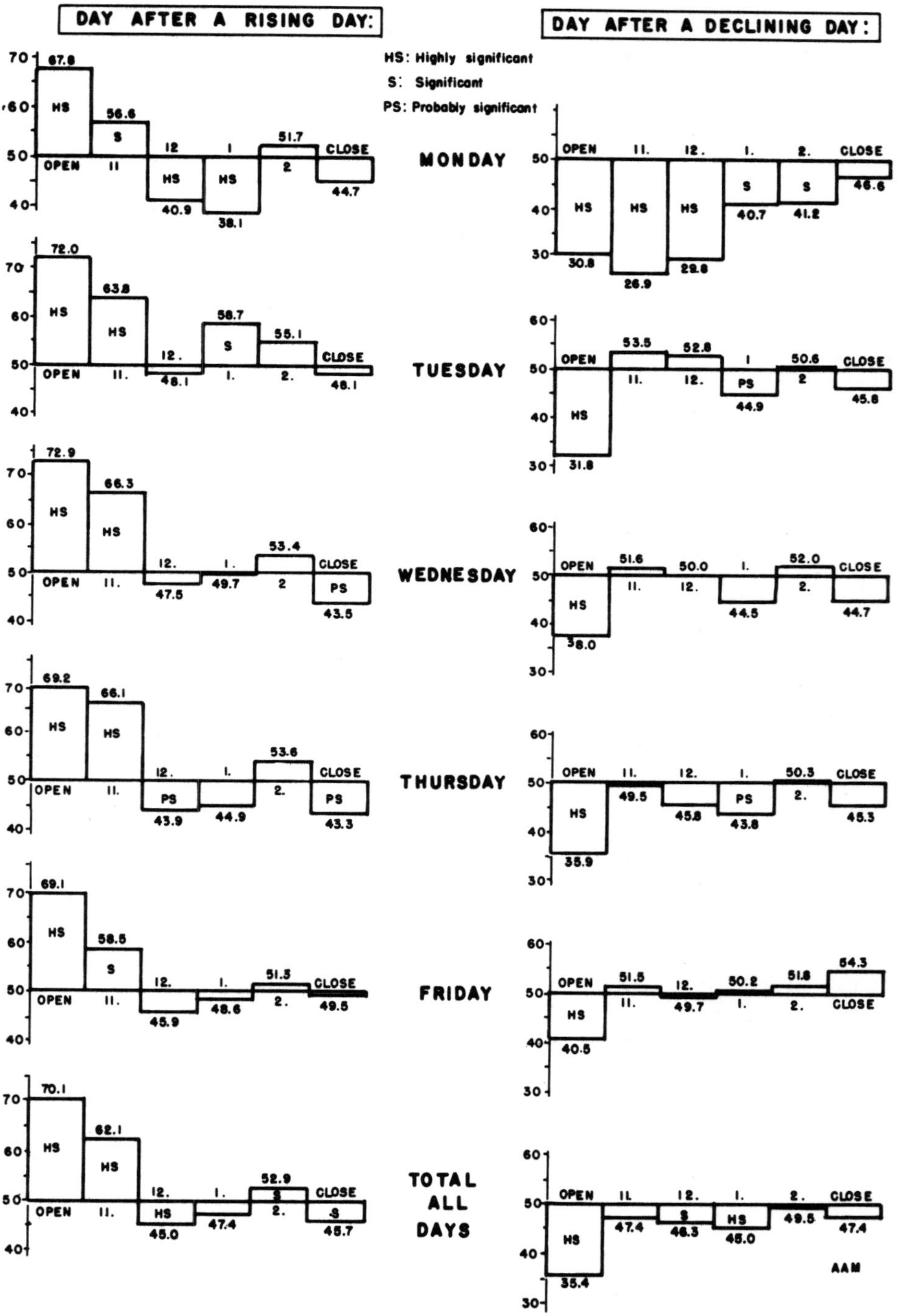

FIG.7.1

7. BEHAVIOR THROUGH THE DAY:

Do buyers tend to predominate in certain hours of the trading day? Do sellers tend to predominate in other specific hours? Does this give the market an upward bias in certain hours, and downward bias in others?

In the first edition of this book, we reported hourly behavior based on a study of every hour in four years. In this second edition we have expanded the data base to every hour in thirteen years. The findings support the original study.

THE OPENING: The first bar in each row of six compares the opening price with the closing price of the previous day. The bar reflects orders placed overnight; these orders, of course, are influenced by investors who watch the market only through newspaper reports. After a rising day the bias is highly significant in an upward direction; after a declining day, the bias is highly significant downward.

THE FIRST HOUR: After a rising day, the bias is definitely upward. This finding should be helpful. If you are planning to buy, for other reasons, place your order at the opening. If you are planning to sell, delay for an hour, and the possibilities favor a better price.

After a declining day, the bias is downward only on Monday. If Friday was weak, and you decide to buy, delay your purchase until after the first hour. Note that the bias continues through most of the day; perhaps you should delay until 2 P.M.! If you plan to sell, sell at the opening.

THE SECOND HOUR: This hour, and the third hour show a downward bias only on Monday. On the remaining days, the bias isn't clear.

The remaining hours of the day don't demonstrate any startling biases.

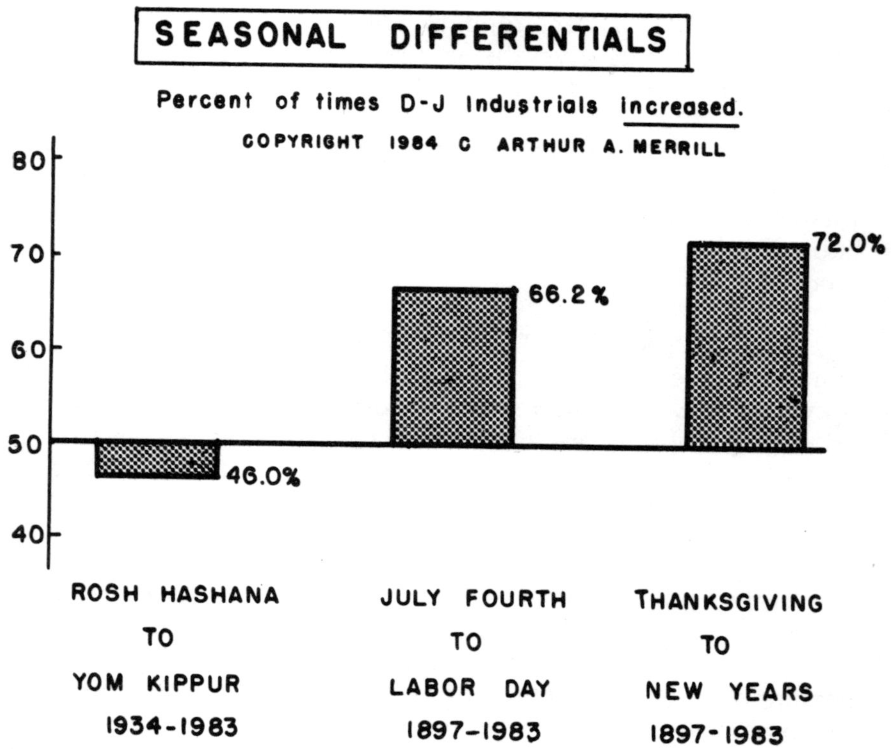
SEASONAL DIFFERENTIALS
Percent of times D-J Industrials increased.
COPYRIGHT 1984 C ARTHUR A. MERRILL
80
70
60
50
40
72.0%
66.2%
46.0%
ROSH HASHANA TO YOM KIPPUR 1934-1983
JULY FOURTH TO LABOR DAY 1897-1983
THANKSGIVING TO NEW YEARS 1897-1983

FIG.8.1

8. BEHAVIOR THROUGH THE SEASONS

Some market sayings are founded on the seasonal tendency. Fig.8.1 reports on three of these seasonal differentials.

The first is "Sell at Rosh Hashana; buy back at Yom Kippur." This is in the midst of the September bearishness.

This saying has been checked back through fifty years. The result is at the left of the chart. The market produced a profitable decline in 54% of the cases, and rose in 46% of the years. This checks the saying, but the difference from expectation isn't statistically significant.

Another saying: "Buy on July Fourth and sell on Labor Day and pay your expenses for the year." This recommendation has been checked for every year back to 1897. The score is good. The market rose in this period, which is the summer rally season, 66.2% of the time. This difference from the average is significant.

We have tried our hand at creating a saying: "Buy at Thanksgiving and sell at New Years and pay your Christmas bills." The score is excellent; the success rate is 72% for the period 1897 through 1983. This is highly significant.

-HOLIDAY BEHAVIOR-

JAN. 1897 - DEC. 1983

(PERCENT OF YEARS IN WHICH THE D-J INDUSTRIALS POSTED AN INCREASE FOR THE DAY--)

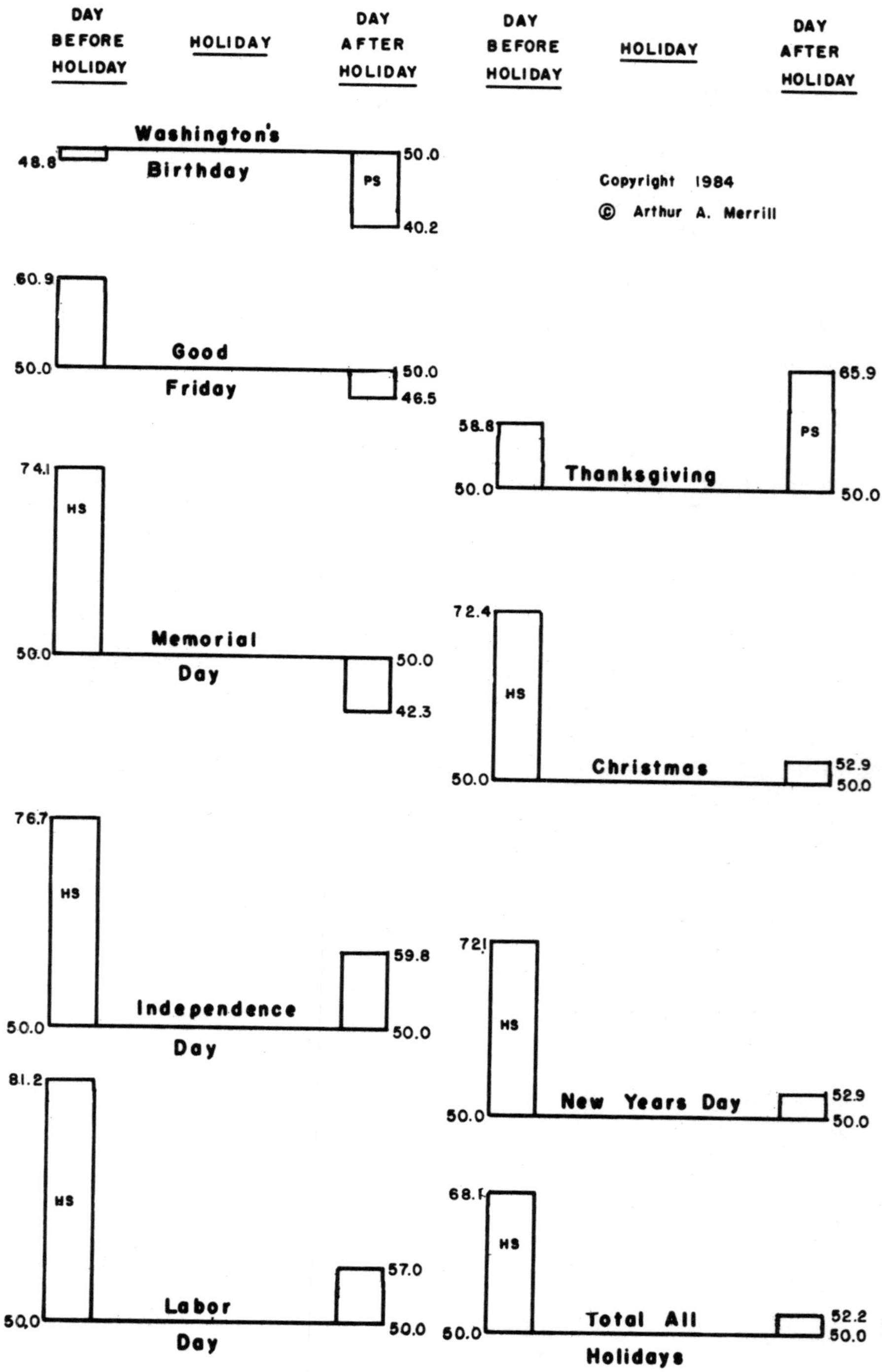

FIG.9.1

9. BEHAVIOR NEAR HOLIDAYS

An erroneous market myth: Traders sell off before a holiday, since they like to be free of worries on the holiday. A clipping in my file : "Market rallies despite holiday- advance runs contrary to the usual pattern of selling before a long weekend." Wrong!

Note Fig.9.1 . It reports on the score of the trading day before and the trading day after each of our current holidays. The record was consulted for almost a hundred years.

Note that the day preceding a holiday is usually a good day. Washington's birthday is an exception, and Thanksgiving is marginal. Overall the market rose 68.1% of the time on the day before a holiday. This is a highly significant score; it would be exceeded by chance only in several thousand repetitions of the history. Note especially the startling ratios on the days preceding Memorial Day, Independence Day, Labor Day, Christmas, and New Year's. Preceding Labor Day the odds are four-to-one.

The trading day after the holidays has a rather poor record. The day after Washington's Birthday is especially bearish. There is one notable exception: the trading day following Thanksgiving is bullish. This may be a reflection of the tendency to rise on a Friday.

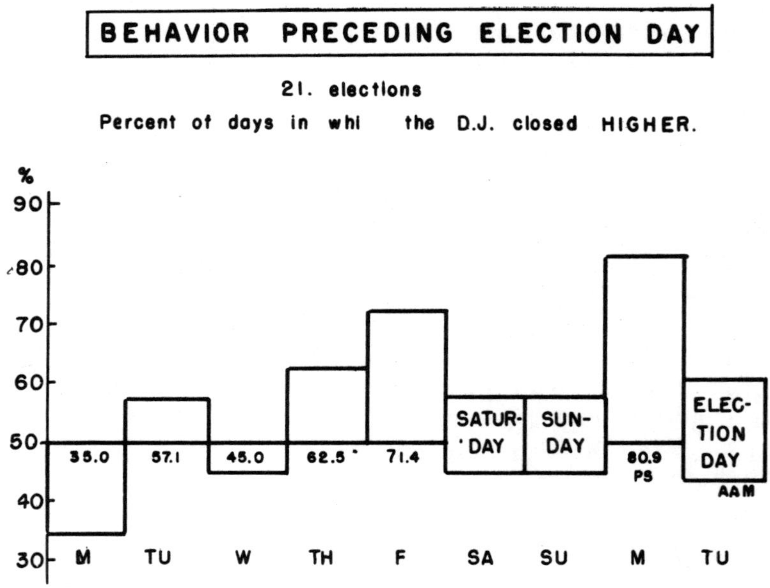
BEHAVIOR PRECEDING ELECTION DAY
21. elections
Percent of days in whi the D.J. closed HIGHER.
%
90
80
70
60
50
40
30
35.0
57.1
45.0
62.5
71.4
SATUR-DAY
SUN-DAY
80.9
PS
ELEC-TION DAY
AAM
M
TU
W
TH
F
SA
SU
M
TU

FIG.9.2

Fig.9.2 charts the behavior in the days preceding election day. The preceding week is typical, with a bearish Monday and bullish Friday.

But the day before election is unusual; instead of the usual blue Monday, it has an extremely bullish record. This day was a rising day seventeen times and a declining day only four times in the last 21 elections.

MARKET ACTION AT TIMES OF BAD NEWS

-DJI CLOSING PRICES, TWO TRADING DAYS PRIOR TO NEWS & FIVE DAYS FOLLOWING-

100% = CLOSING PRIOR TO NEWS--

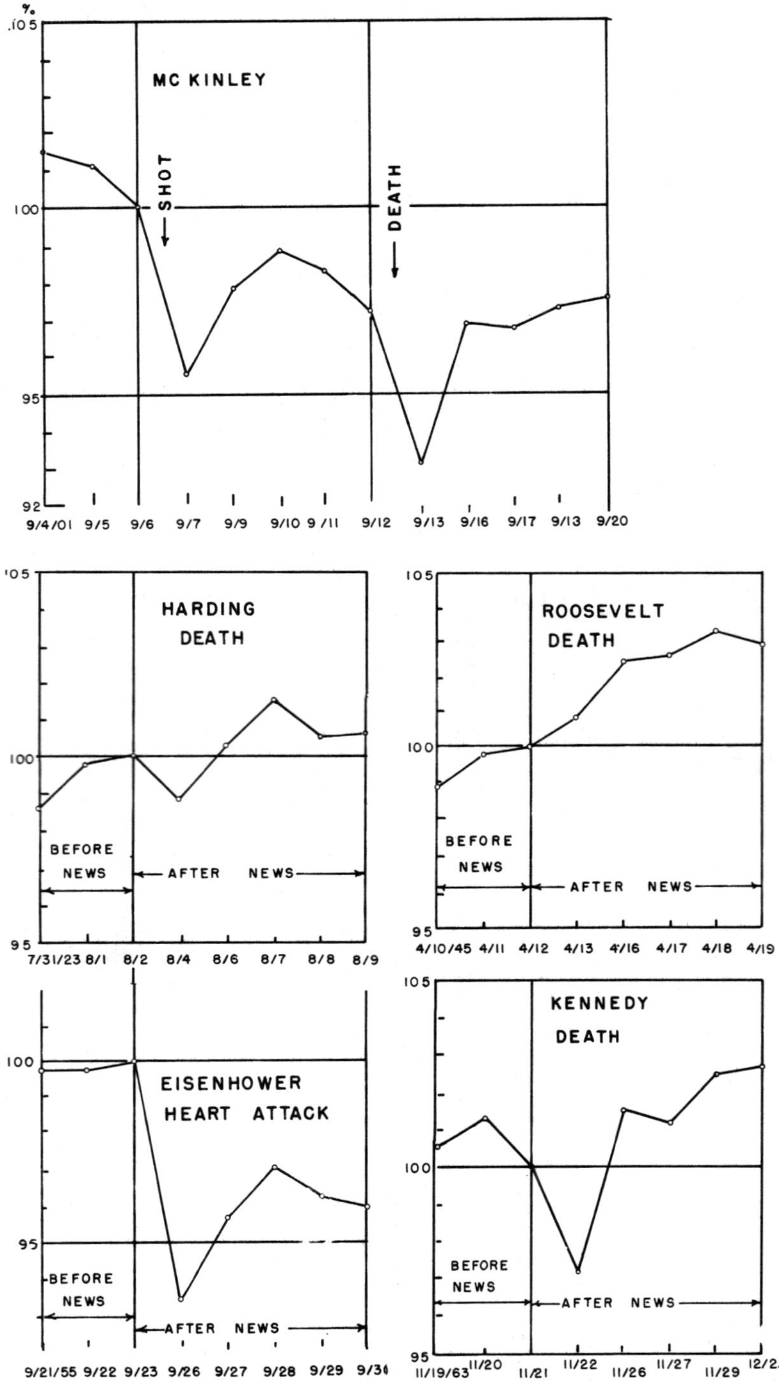

FIG.10.1

10. BEHAVIOR WHEN NEWS BREAKS

From the viewpoint of the market, news can be categorized as predictable or nonpredictable.

When predictable news occurs, the market has already discounted its effects. If some good predictable news breaks, the market often declines rather than advances; acute investors are taking their profits. The reverse is true when predictable bad news appears.

Unpredictable news is another matter. Fig.10.1 charts the market behavior after five cases of tragic news. The market had some bad moments immediately following the news. Selling drove prices down to a surprising degree. However, when a day has passed, the market recovers from its panic and sometimes works upward to a higher level.

BEHAVIOR AFTER A CHANGE IN THE DISCOUNT RATE

96 Changes: 1933-1983

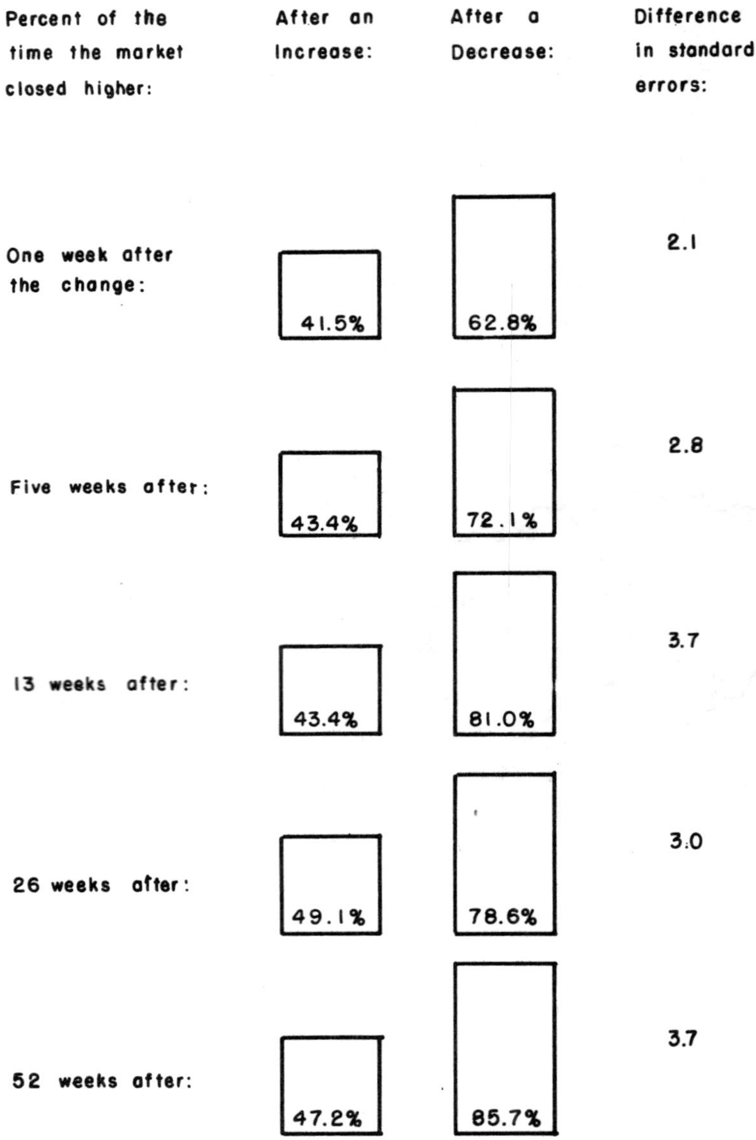

Example: The market (DJ Industrials) closed higher 72.1% of the time five weeks after a discount rate decrease. AAM

2. std. errors: Probably significant. 3. std. errors: Highly significant.

FIG. 11.1

11. BEHAVIOR AFTER A MOVE BY THE FEDERAL RESERVE:

The Federal Reserve was created to improve the credit conditions in our country. It was given several powers to assist it in this work, including the ability to tighten or ease credit. The powers were given to the Federal Reserve to encourage stability and health in our money markets.

Four of the actions by the Fed can be watched easily:

1.The discount rate, or the rate at which members can rediscount paper at the Federal Reserve.

2.The margin requirements for stock purchases.

3.The amount of reserves the member banks must carry with the Federal Reserve Banks.

4.The open market purchase and sale of government securities. The result of this action can be monitored by watching the balance of free reserves in the system, and the tightness of credit as reflected by the Federal Funds rate.

BEHAVIOR AFTER A CHANGE IN THE DISCOUNT RATE:

The historical record for the last 20 years is in Figs.11.3.11.4, and 11.5.

In the fifty years 1933 through 1983 there were 96 discount rate changes. Note Fig.11.1 . The left hand bars report what happened to the Dow in the period following an increase in the discount rate. As expected, an increase, which tightens credit, was negative. The market closed higher less than 50% of the time one week later, five weeks later, and 13, 26, and 52 weeks later.

The right hand bars report what happened following a decrease in the discount rate. The action, which eases credit, was positive. The market closed higher much more often after discount rate decreases. After six months, the probability of higher stock prices is about four-to-one.

The significance of the difference between the performance after an increase and the scores after a decrease is measured by the right hand column of "standard errors." A difference of two standard errors is considered probably significant; three standard errors is highly significant.

BEHAVIOR AFTER A CHANGE IN RESERVE REQUIREMENTS

34. changes 1936-1975

Percent of the time the market closed higher:	After an Increase:	After a Decrease	Difference in standard errors:
One week after the change:	50.0%	63,6%	0.8
Five weeks after:	66.7%	72.7%	0.4
13. weeks after:	66.7%	86.4%	1.4
26. weeks after:	66.7%	100.0%	2.9
52. weeks after:	58.3%	95.5%	2.7

Example: The market (DJ Industrials) closed higher 72.7% of the time five weeks after a decrease in reserve requirements
2 std.errors: Probably significant. 3. std.errors: Highly significant. AAM

FIG.11.2

BEHAVIOR AFTER A CHANGE IN MARGIN REQUIREMENTS:

This behavior was analyzed with a method similar to Fig. 11.1, but the results didn't prove significant.

BEHAVIOR AFTER A CHANGE IN RESERVE REQUIREMENTS:

Fig.11.2 reports the average behavior after 34 reserve requirement changes.

Note the right hand column. The standard errors didn't show significant behavior until six months after the change. For the longer term, the behavior after an increase is significantly different from behavior after a decrease. The market rose more often, as expected, after an ease in reserve requirements.

BEHAVIOR AFTER A CHANGE IN FREE RESERVES:

To make this check, free reserves were tracked through the five year period from 1979 through 1983. The figures were smoothed by various moving averages. The most successful combination found was the difference between the five week and 52 week averages. (Equivalent exponential averages were used.) When this difference exceeded 235 million (2/3 of a standard deviation), the difference was rated "high"; when below minus 235 it was rated "low". The success of these "high" or "low" figures in calling the direction of the market in the five year test period was:

weeks later	percent accuracy	chi squared	
1	55.1	0.9	
5	60.8	4.5	probably significant
13	68.2	13.5	highly significant
26	67.3	12.1	highly significant
52	81.6	39.8	highly significant

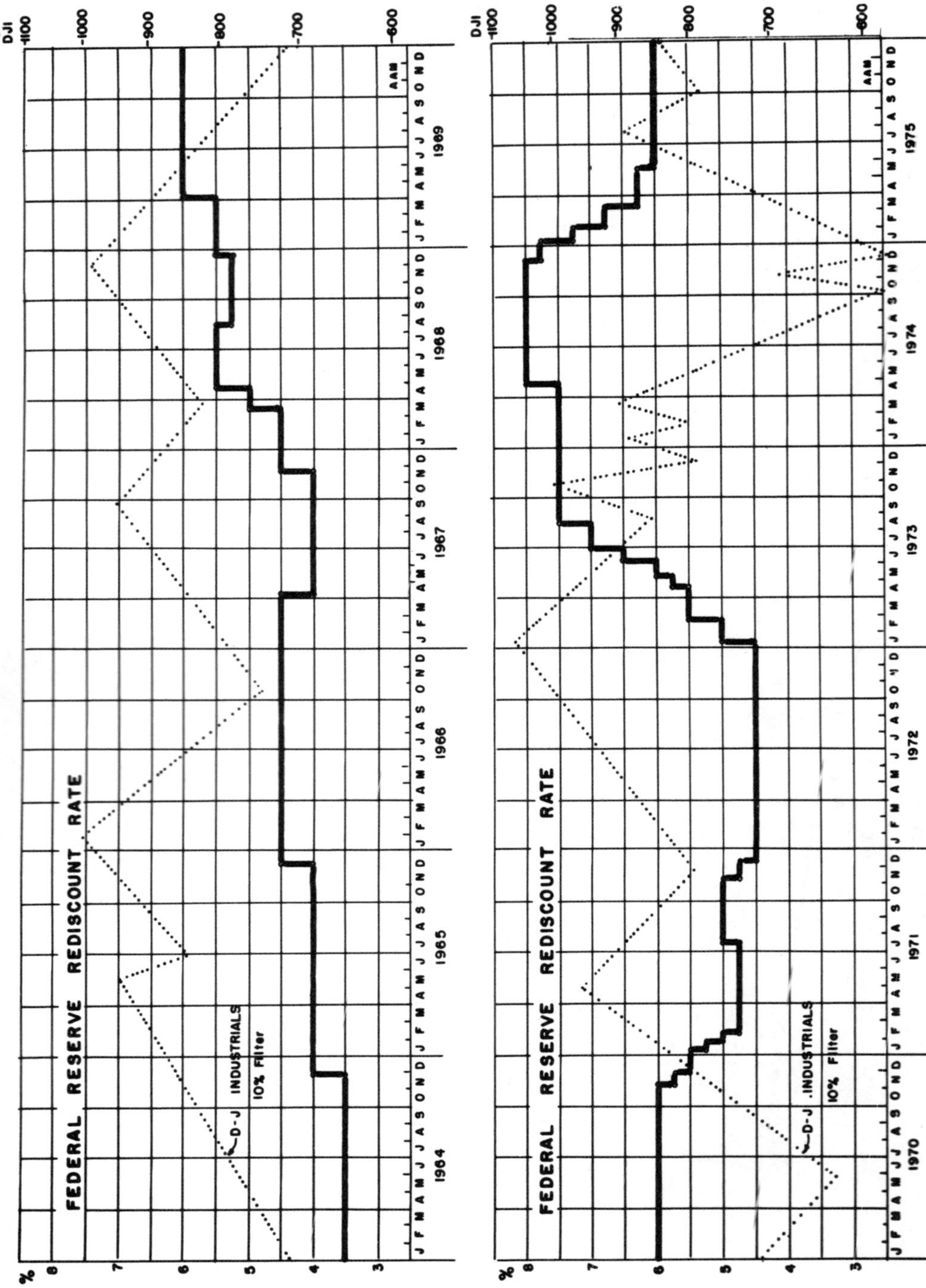
FEDERAL RESERVE REDISCOUNT RATE
D-J INDUSTRIALS
10% Filter
DJI
%
AAM
1964
1965
1966
1967
1968
1969
1970
1971
1972
1973
1974
1975

FIG.11.3

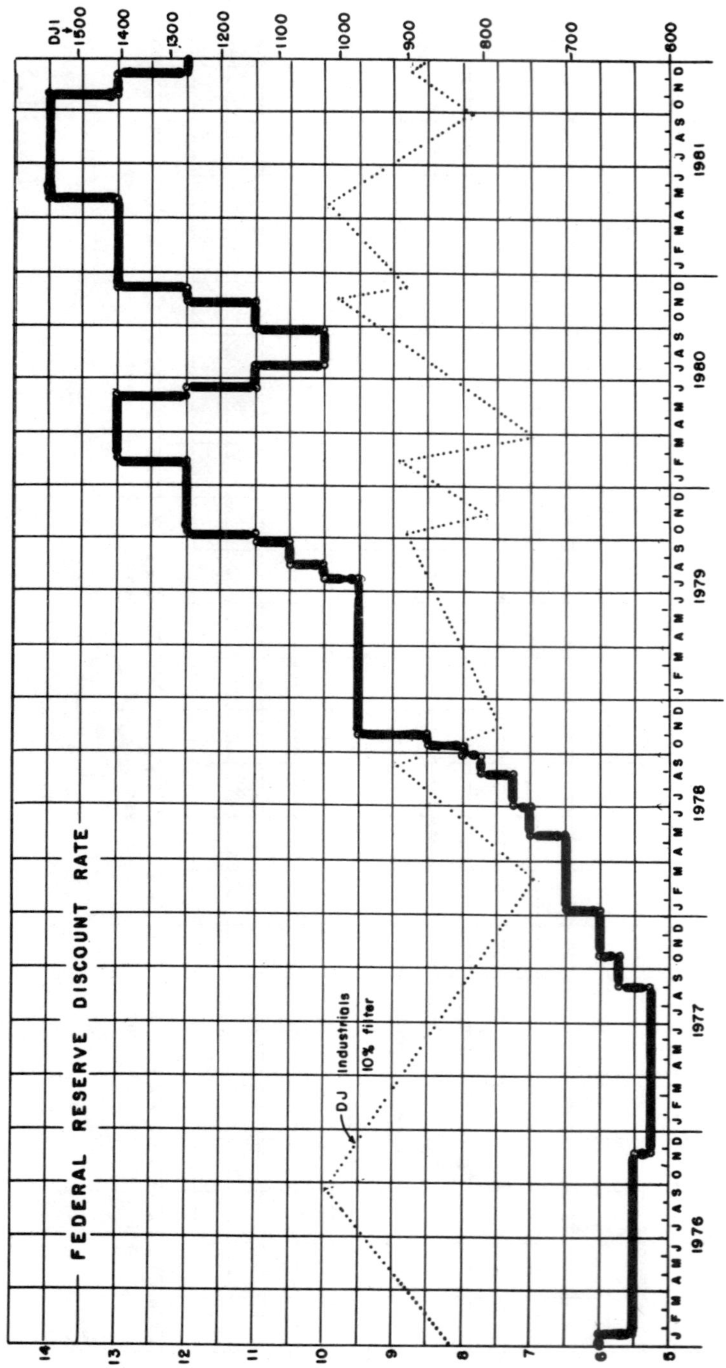
FEDERAL RESERVE DISCOUNT RATE
DJ Industrials
10% filter
DJI
1976
1977
1978
1979
1980
1981

FIG.11.4

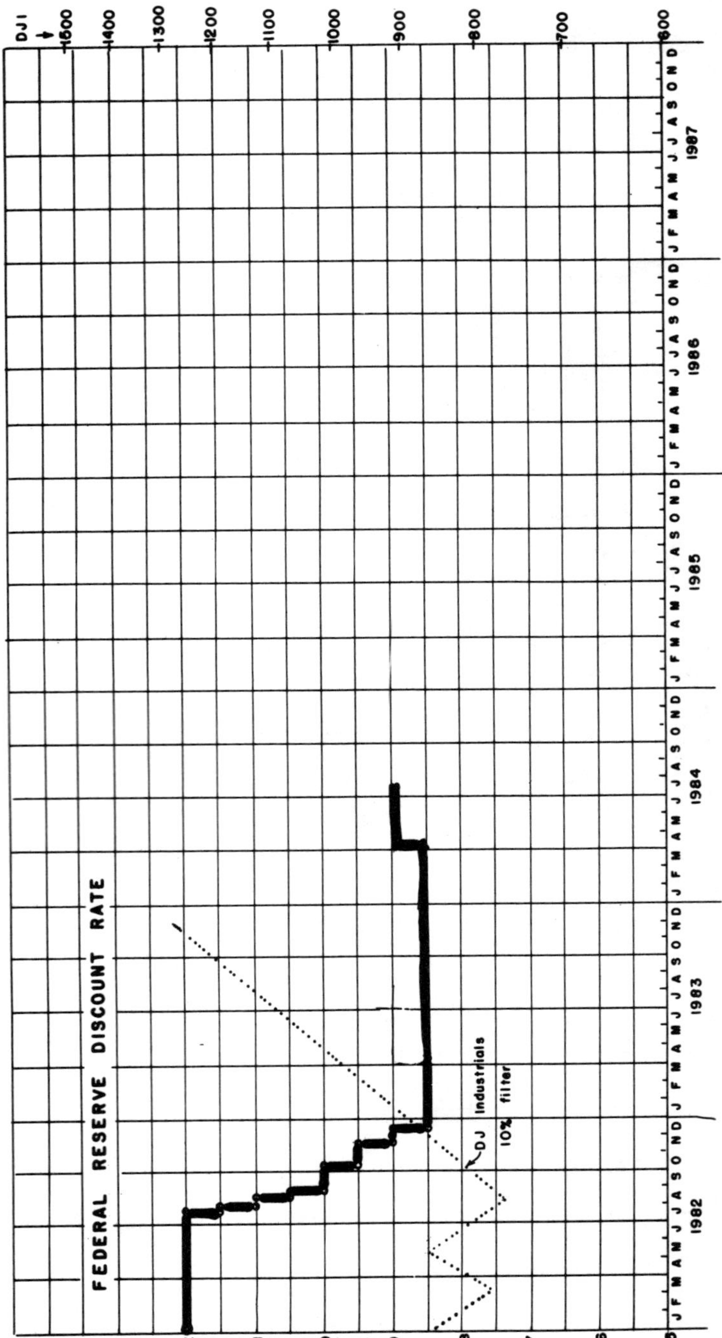
FEDERAL RESERVE DISCOUNT RATE
DJI
1500
1400
1300
1200
1100
1000
900
800
700
600
14
13
12
11
10
9
8
7
6
5
DJ Industrials
10% filter
J F M A M J J A S O N D
1982
1983
1984
1985
1986
1987

FIG.11.5

12. BEHAVIOR NEAR SUPPORT OR RESISTANCE:

Analysts have found that previous turning points often prove to be levels where buying appears to resist a downswing, or selling appears to resist an upswing. Examples can be found in double tops and bottoms, and also in horizontal trend channels when prices meander between an upper resistance level and a lower support level.

Support and resistance can vary within the space of a single point. This tendency is summarized in Fig.12.1, which requires some explanation.

All of the common stocks on the N.Y. Exchange were examined in 1961, 1962 and again in 1983. The top of a bull market occurred in 1961; the bottom of a bear market in 1962. The top of a major swing occurred in 1983. The resultant findings in the later year supported the earlier years. The chart combines all of the data.

In the upper part of the chart, the high points of the years were noted. Only the fraction at the end of the price was tabulated. For example, a stock with a high for the year of 67 would be in the upper bar; one with a high of 6 7/8 would be in the next bar; one with a high of 26 3/4 would be in the third bar.

Note that the even number is a strong resistance level. 22.3% of the stocks topped out at the even price. The next most popular resistance was at the 1/2, with 18.6%. The quarter point follow; the eighths are least popular.

Stock seems to be offered for sale more often at the even price; the half is almost as big a resistance level. If you plan to sell at the top, then you should avoid offering at the eighth, since the price will probably move up to the next quarter.

The reverse, of course, is true on a stop-loss. These should be placed on the eighth points, since prices will probably not stop at the eighth, but will move higher.

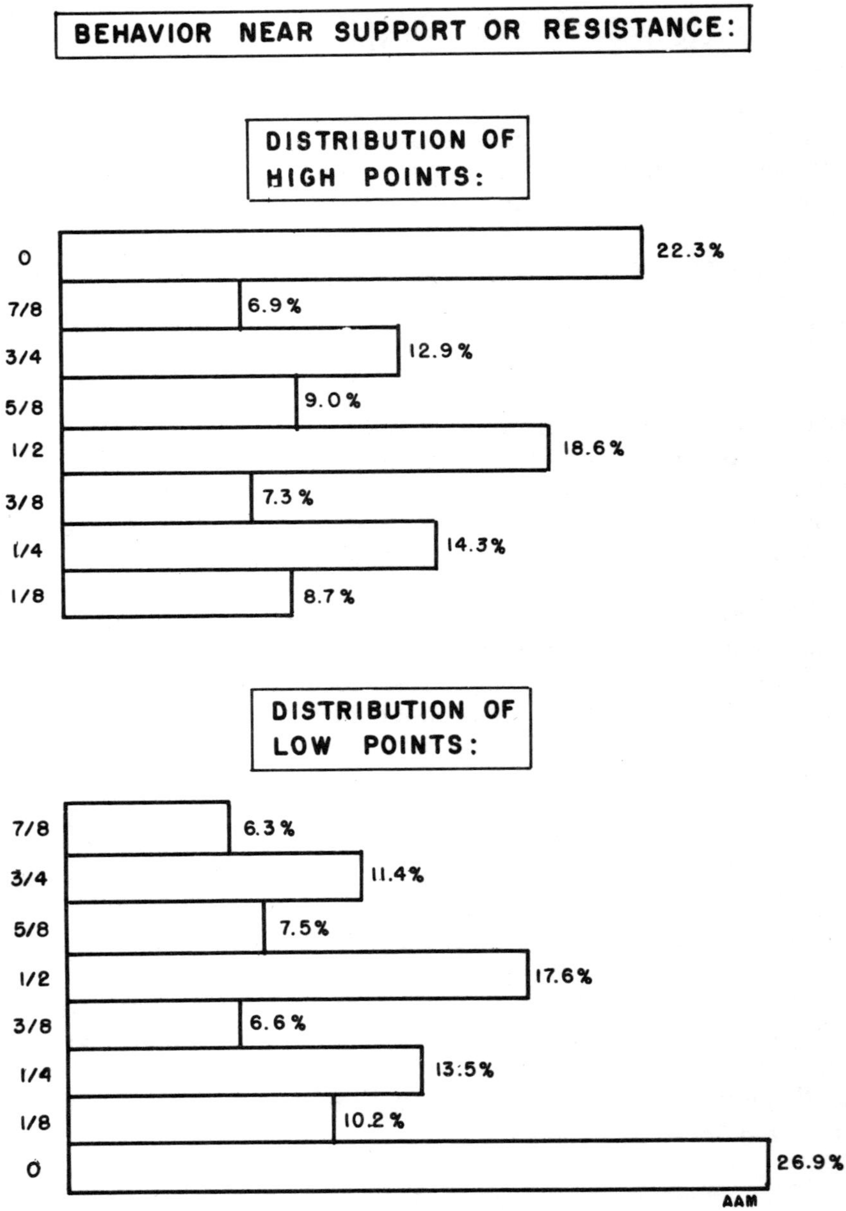
BEHAVIOR NEAR SUPPORT OR RESISTANCE:
DISTRIBUTION OF HIGH POINTS:
0
22.3%
7/8
6.9%
3/4
12.9%
5/8
9.0%
1/2
18.6%
3/8
7.3%
1/4
14.3%
1/8
8.7%
DISTRIBUTION OF LOW POINTS:
7/8
6.3%
3/4
11.4%
5/8
7.5%
1/2
17.6%
3/8
6.6%
1/4
13.5%
1/8
10.2%
0
26.9%
AAM

FIG.12.1

Consider the lower half of Fig.12.1 . The low price of all common stocks on the NYSE was noted and tabulated. The even price, again, is the most important support. 26.9% of the stocks stopped their decline at an even price. A lot of purchase orders seem to be placed at this price. The next most important support point is the half, where 17.6% of the stocks stopped their decline.

For profit on purchase, then, one should not place purchase points at the 1/8 level, since they will probably continue down to the next even quarter before reversing. For stop loss, the reverse is true. This order should be on the eighths, since a price will probably continue to the next quarter. The 7/8 point (just below major support) should be a good place for a stop loss.

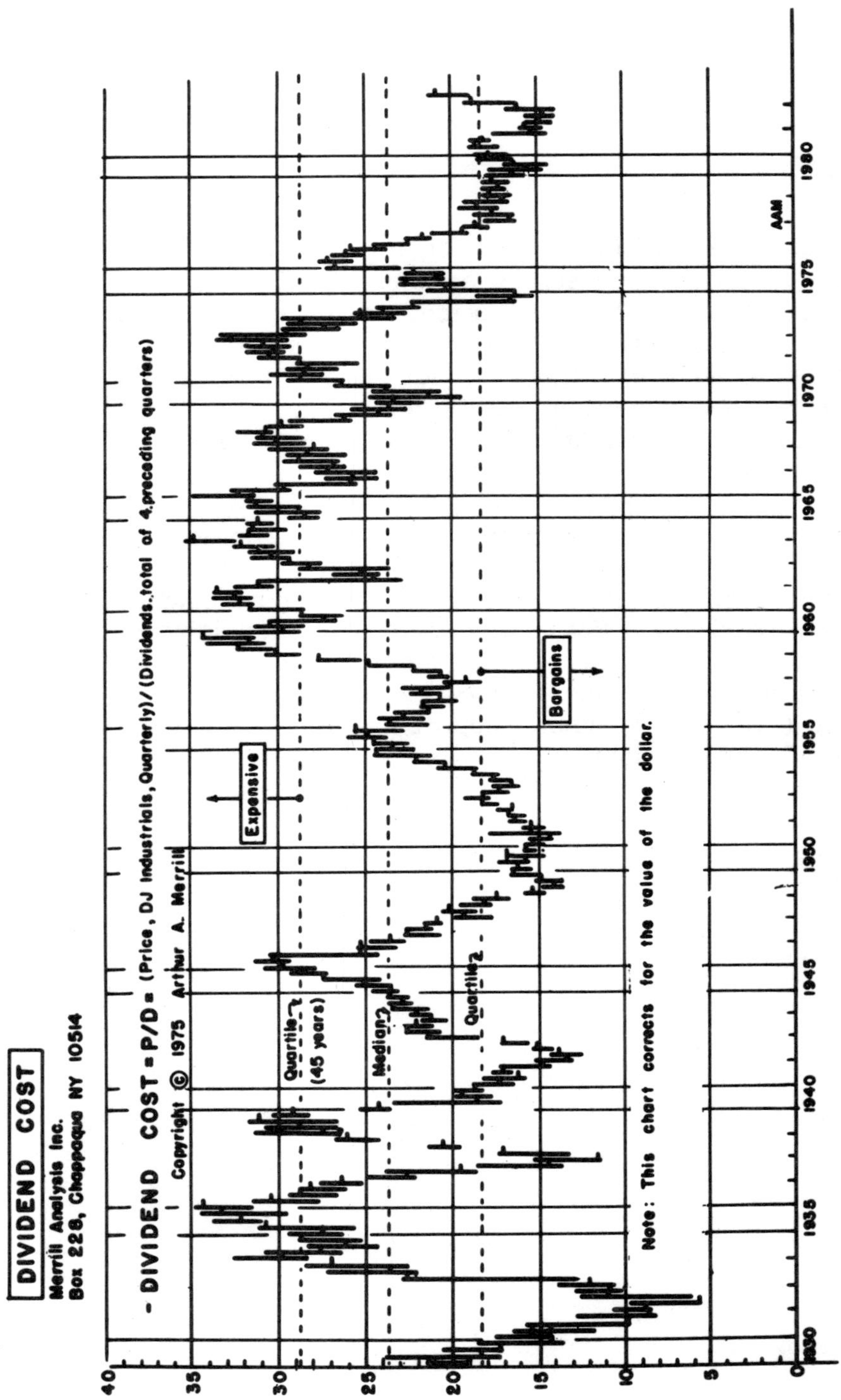
DIVIDEND COST
Merrill Analysis Inc.
Box 228, Chappaqua NY 10514
- DIVIDEND COST = P/D = (Price, DJ Industrials, Quarterly)/(Dividends, total of 4 preceding quarters)
Copyright © 1975 Arthur A. Merrill
Quartile
(45 years)
Median
Quartile
Expensive
Bargains
Note: This chart corrects for the value of the dollar.
AAM
40
35
30
25
20
15
10
5
0
1930
1935
1940
1945
1950
1955
1960
1965
1970
1975
1980

FIG.13.1

13. BEHAVIOR RELATIVE TO DIVIDENDS:

Stock prices should be founded solidly on earnings and prospective earnings. The dividend rate is founded on earnings and prospective earnings. The syllogism closes; stock prices should be founded, or related to, the dividend rate.

Investors, however, have been willing, at some times in the past, to sell Dow stocks valued at less than $10 per dollar of dividends; they have at other times been willing to spend more than $30 to receive one dollar of dividends.

Fig.13.1 illustrated this variation. The cost of one dollar of dividends is obtained by dividing the DJ Industrials yield into 100, or by dividing price by the dividends in the preceding four quarters.

Note that the chart corrects for the value of the dollar. Both price and dividends include the effects of inflation; since the chart is a ratio of price to dividends, the inflation effect cancels out. On a short term, the correction isn't perfect, since prices reflect change in the value of the dollar more rapidly than dividends.

The horizontal dashed lines have been placed to divide the points in the chart into four approximately equal parts (the quartiles). In the upper quarter, investors have been willing to pay more than $28.80 to get one dollar of dividends. This area is labeled "expensive."

The central dashed line is at $23.80 . This is the average for the entire period covered by the chart. The lower dashed line is at $18.30 . The area below this line is labeled "Bargain."

These bench marks can be translated into levels of the DJ Industrials by multiplying by the dividends paid in the preceding four quarters. For example, in July 1984 the dividends paid in the four quarters preceding June 30 totaled $57.67 for the Dow Industrial stocks. Multiplying this dividend rate by the chart bench mark levels gives the following result:

Above 1660 :	Expensive
At 1372:	Reasonably priced
Below 1055:	Bargains

This is a useful chart. When we published in earlier years, when prices were in the "expensive" area, we commented "this chart gives us nightmares." In the first edition of this book, in 1966, we noted that prices were in the expensive area. In the September 13, 1974 issue of the report "Technical Trends", I reported that "prices have dropped into the 'Bargain' area for the first time in twenty years."

A technical student will note wide gaps; these are the result of changes in dividends.

(Statistical notes: The D-J Company has reported dividends back through 1929. Since we use "preceding", we could carry the ratios back through 1930. An earlier tabulation of yields indicates a peak of P/D of $34.70 in 1929. It should be noted that the D-J reports of dividends unfortunately include stock dividends. In the 1930-1938 period, annual figures of dividends only were available; we estimated the quarterly figures by interpolation. The quartile distribution is based on monthly closing prices.)

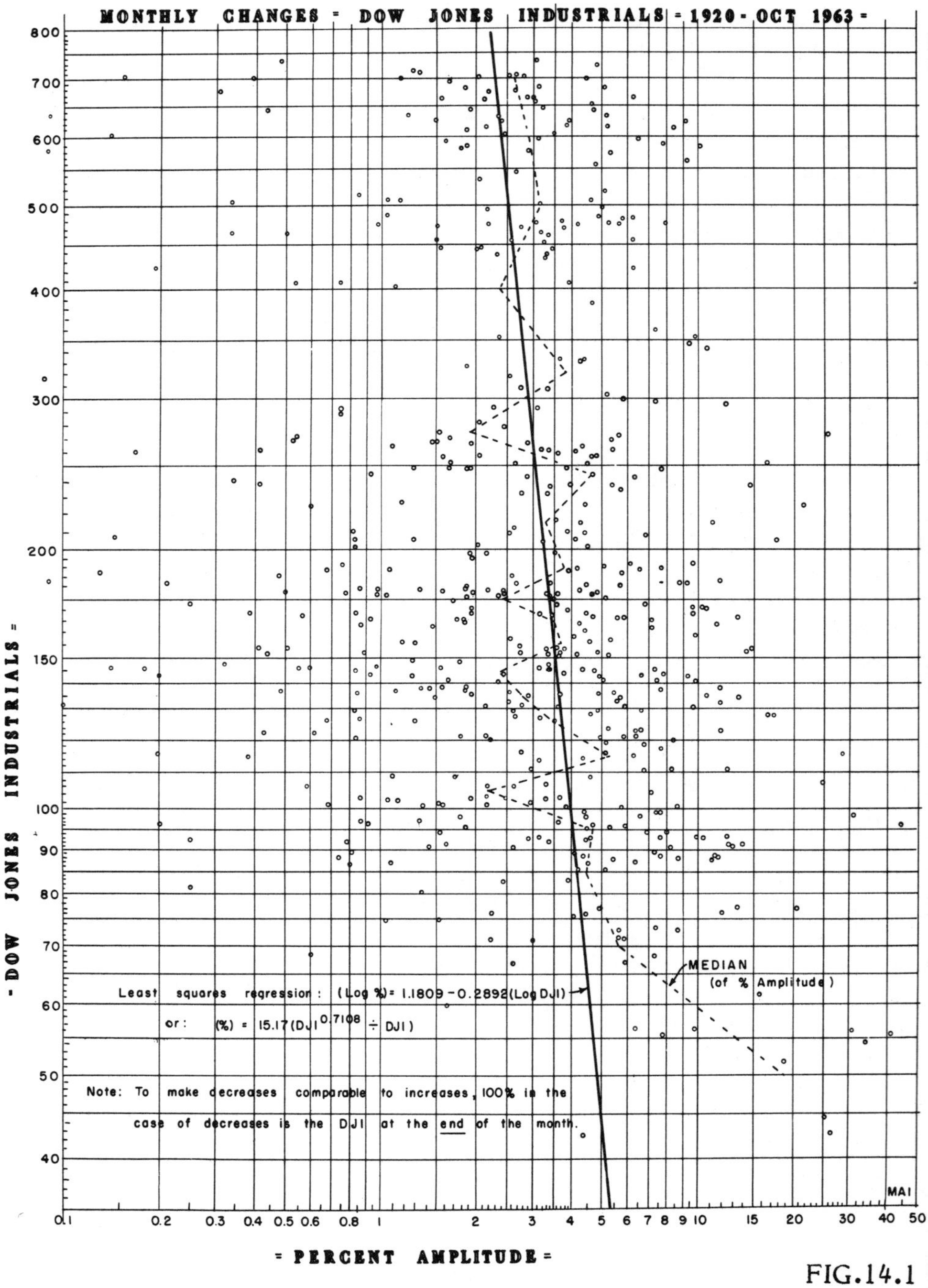
MONTHLY CHANGES = DOW JONES INDUSTRIALS = 1920 - OCT 1963 =
- DOW JONES INDUSTRIALS =
= PERCENT AMPLITUDE =
MEDIAN
(of % Amplitude)
Least squares regression: (Log %) = 1.1809 - 0.2892 (Log DJI)
or: (%) = 15.17 (DJI^0.7108 ÷ DJI)
Note: To make decreases comparable to increases, 100% in the case of decreases is the DJI at the end of the month.
MAI

FIG. 14.1

14. BEHAVIOR AS INFLUENCED BY PRICE:

Stocks with low prices seem to move up and down, percentagewise, more rapidly than high priced stocks. Some observers have concluded that the variations tend to change with the square root of the price.

In Fig.14.1, the monthly percentage changes of the DJ Industrials, for each month over a 43 year period, are charted against the level of the averages.

The percent changes tend to be higher at the lower price levels, as expected. A median line (dashed) traces this tendency. The relationship isn't close, however, and the data are scattered.

A least squares line (the solid line) casts some doubt on the square root relationship. The square root is expressed as a 0.5 root; the calculation suggests 0.71 as the correct value.

RUNS- - - WEEKS

58 Years 1926-1983

Probability that a run will continue in the same direction and not reverse.

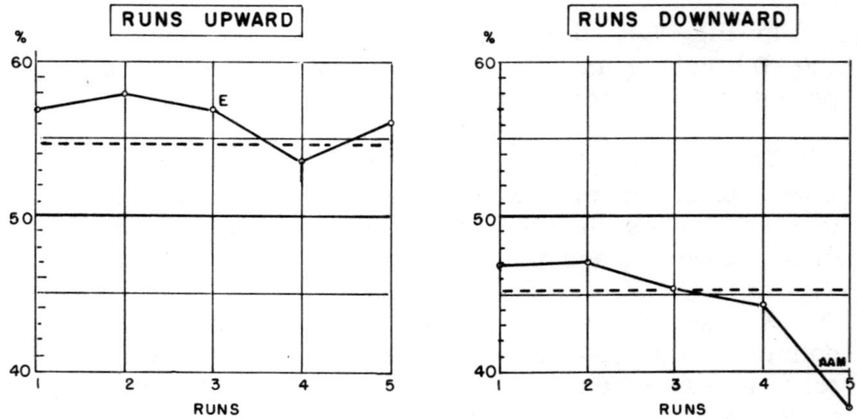

FIG.15.1

15. BEHAVIOR IN RUNS:

If you flip a coin, and get five heads in a row, the chance for a sixth head is still fifty-fifty, since the coin has no memory.

But the market has a memory. What are the chances for another rise after five rises in a row? After five consecutive declines?

WEEKLY RUNS:

Fig.15.1 reports the score for weekly runs, based on 58 years of history. The chart shows the percent of the occasions that the market continued in the same direction, and didn't reverse.

For example, suppose that the Dow has risen three weeks in a row. What is the probability of another rise, making it four in a row? In all weeks in the 58 year period, 54.5% were rising weeks. This is the dashed line on the left hand chart. After runs of three weeks, in the test period, 57% of the weeks following were rising weeks (point E), which is slightly higher than the average (54.5%).

For runs upward, there seems to be a slight tendency to continue, but this isn't enough to be statistically significant.

In the downward direction there seems to be a tendency to reverse after a run of five, but this still isn't statistically significant.

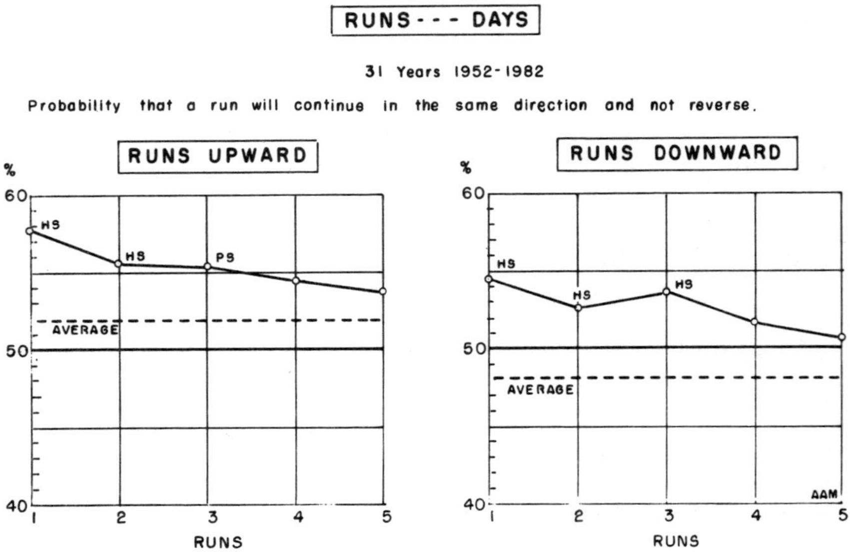

FIG.15.2

DAILY RUNS:

Fig. 15.2 reports the score for daily runs, based on 30 years.

Here we have some highly significant scores. The chance is less than one in a thousand that this would be a chance score.

But don't get excited. The percentage probability for a continuation is only 55% in the up direction and 53% in the down direction. This isn't far from fifty-fifty.

RUNS --- HOURS

Probability that a run will continue in the same direction and not reverse. (Data base: 7 years)

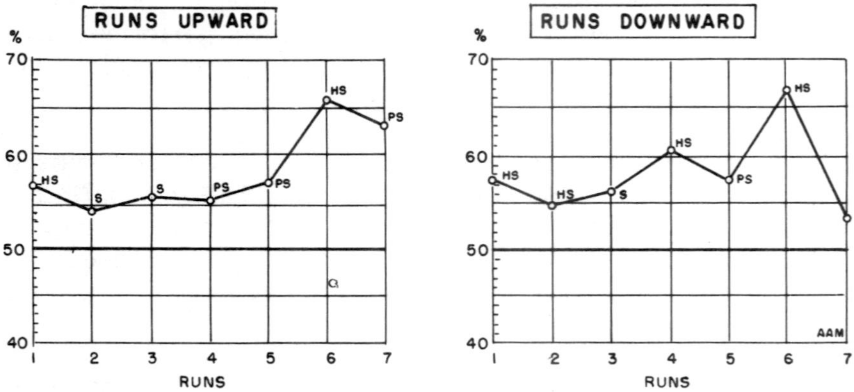

FIG.15.3

HOURLY RUNS:

Fig. 15.3 reports the scores for hourly runs. This is beginning to look useful.

Some of the scores are significant; some are highly significant. The probabilities are now up to 65% (two to one odds) for some of the longer runs.

16. BEHAVIOR IN PATTERNS:

The market swings up and down in waves. Do some of these patterns repeat? How has the market performed after the pattern? Is the behavior after the pattern significantly bullish or significantly bearish?

To answer these questions definitely, a pattern must be defined sufficiently so that repetitions can be definitely recognized. Then the behavior after the pattern can be noted, counted, reduced to numbers and checked for significance. Lord Kelvin's dictum, quoted at the beginning of this book, can be satisfied.

There have been several attempts to codify patterns. Unfortunately, they usually are stated in general terms, and require interpretation and judgment; reduction to numbers for testing is frustrated.

Some of the methods are listed below. The first four require judgment; the last three are definite and can be tested.

1.BAR CHARTS: These are the familiar charts with vertical lines connecting the high price and the low price for each day or week. "Formations" or shapes made by the bars have been named; "triangles","double tops","head and shoulders" are examples. Since the interpretation requires judgment, this book won't go into details. For an authoritative discussion see Edwards and Magee "Technical Analysis of Stock Trends"(see App.J).

2.POINT AND FIGURE CHARTS: This is a popular method of charting; but formations are in general terms and won't be discussed in this book. For one good source see Alexander and Whelan "Study Helps" (App.J.)

3.DOW THEORY: This theory is outlined in Appendix C. Unfortunately, this is also stated in general terms. Dow Theorists will argue, with no clear conclusions, about the validity of a support level. Is it , or is it not, important enough to make its violation a sign of a change of trend?

4.ELLIOTT WAVE THEORY: This is outlined in Appendix D. I have tried to read Elliott's mind, by analyzing his own classification of the record, but it was a frustrating endeavor. Some of his minor waves appeared to be bigger than waves of the next higher classification; some prominent turning points were omitted. Since judgment is required for interpretation, a student should check his classification against that of a qualified expert. Currently the outstanding authority is Robert Prechter of Gainesville Ga.

5.MW WAVES: Here is a definite classification. If a filter is used to set a minimum size of a swing, the remaining waves can be definitely classified and tested. This classification will be discussed in the next chapter.

6.TIME PATTERNS: Here another definite classification is proposed. If the direction of a move, and not its magnitude, is considered in a prescribed time frame, a definite classification is possible and can be tested. This classification will be described in chapter 18.

7.CYCLES: Is there an underlying regularity hidden in the irregular swings of stock prices? This will be the subject of chapter 19.

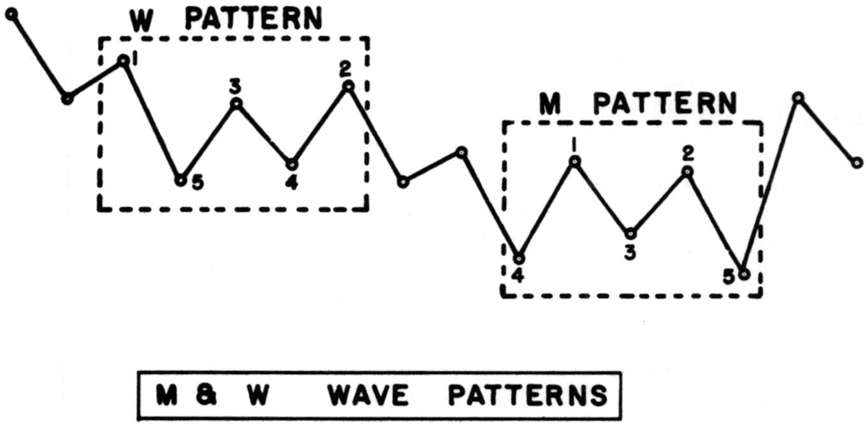

FIG.17.1

17. BEHAVIOR IN M AND W PATTERNS

If minor fluctuations are ignored or filtered out, and the resultant turning points are connected by straight lines, the resultant zigzag patterns can be classified.

Pick any five consecutive turning points. If the first swing is downward, the pattern forms a W. Note Fig.17.1 . If the first swing is upward, the pattern forms an M. There are 32 possible patterns, which I have classified in Fig.17.2 and 17.3 as 16 M waves and 16 waves.

Are some of these patterns bullish? Are some bearish? When a certain pattern occurred in the past, what happened to prices after the pattern?

In 1971 Robert Levy suggested identifying patterns of five consecutive turning points by ranking the points in the pattern from one for the highest down to five for the lowest. If these rank numbers are read from left to to right, a five digit identifying label is produced. These identifying labels are below each of the patterns in Figs.17.2 and 17.3 .

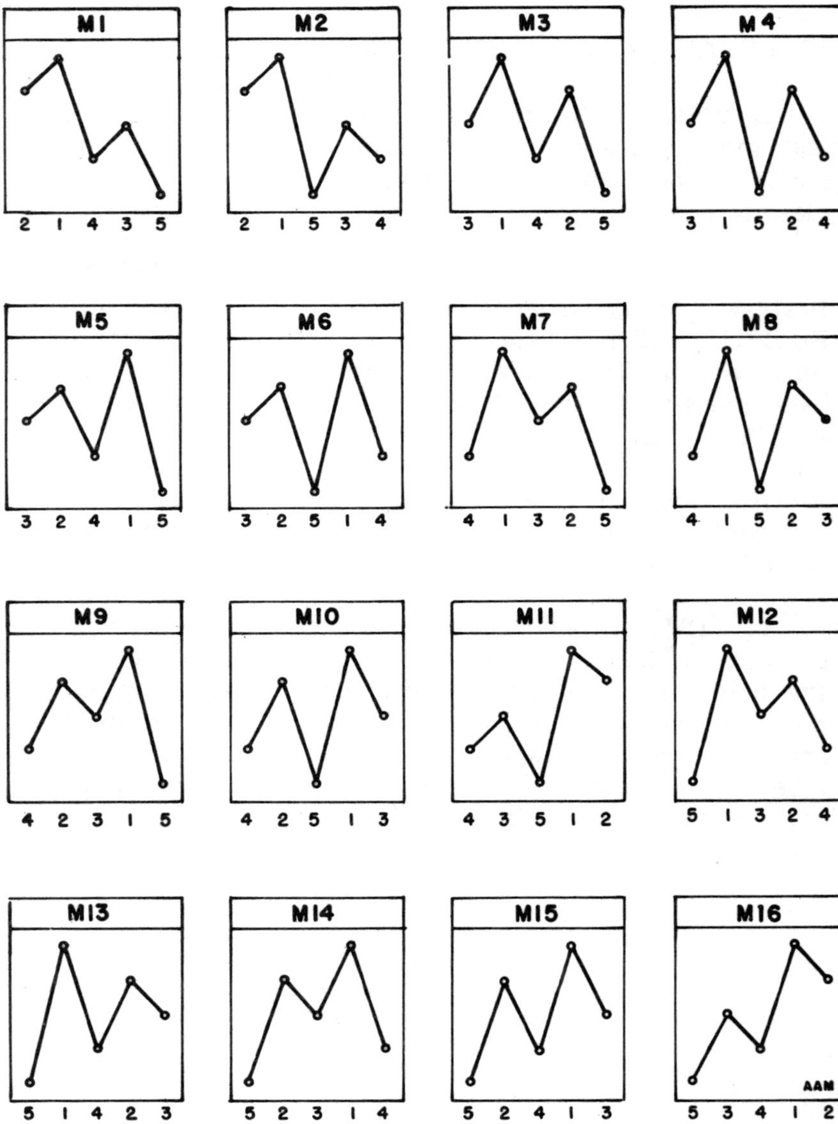
M1
2 1 4 3 5
M2
2 1 5 3 4
M3
3 1 4 2 5
M4
3 1 5 2 4
M5
3 2 4 1 5
M6
3 2 5 1 4
M7
4 1 3 2 5
M8
4 1 5 2 3
M9
4 2 3 1 5
M10
4 2 5 1 3
M11
4 3 5 1 2
M12
5 1 3 2 4
M13
5 1 4 2 3
M14
5 2 3 1 4
M15
5 2 4 1 3
M16
AAM
5 3 4 1 2

FIG.17.2

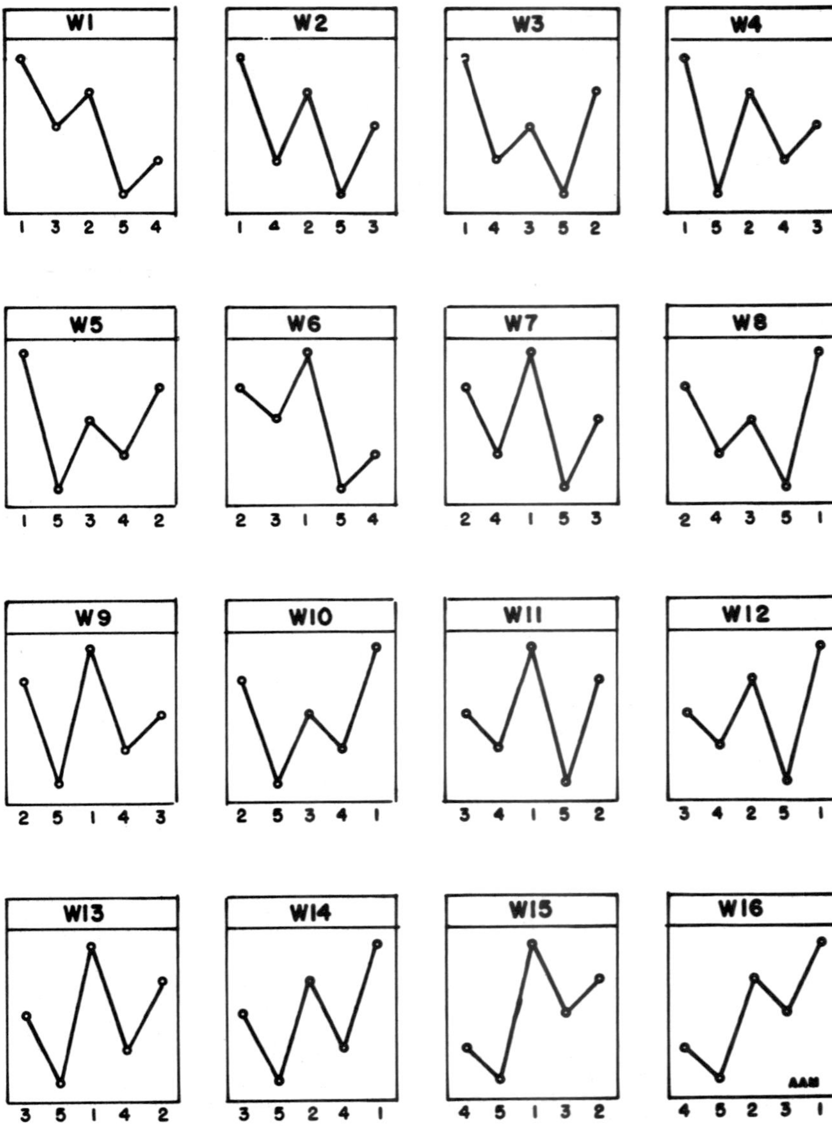
W1
1 3 2 5 4
W2
1 4 2 5 3
W3
1 4 3 5 2
W4
1 5 2 4 3
W5
1 5 3 4 2
W6
2 3 1 5 4
W7
2 4 1 5 3
W8
2 4 3 5 1
W9
2 5 1 4 3
W10
2 5 3 4 1
W11
3 4 1 5 2
W12
3 4 2 5 1
W13
3 5 1 4 2
W14
3 5 2 4 1
W15
4 5 1 3 2
W16
4 5 2 3 1
AAM

FIG.17.3

M WAVES

WAVE		UP	DWN	%UP	
M	1	24	33	42.11	●
M	2	15	22	40.54	●
M	3	68	42	61.82	
M	4	37	34	52.11	
M	5	19	20	48.72	
M	6	10	13	43.48	
M	7	38	16	70.37	●
M	8	14	7	66.67	
M	9	24	24	50.00	
M	10	25	16	60.98	
M	11	23	22	51.11	
M	12	42	30	58.33	
M	13	40	15	72.73	●
M	14	29	22	56.86	
M	15	105	80	56.76	
M	16	64	36	64.00	

W WAVES

WAVE		UP	DWN	%UP	
W	1	34	30	53.13	
W	2	66	59	52.80	
W	3	30	26	53.57	
W	4	26	7	78.79	●
W	5	36	31	53.73	
W	6	14	15	48.28	
W	7	33	29	53.23	
W	8	27	29	48.21	
W	9	16	10	61.54	
W	10	47	33	58.75	
W	11	11	7	61.11	
W	12	18	21	46.15	
W	13	48	29	62.34	
W	14	84	62	57.53	
W	15	27	22	55.10	
W	16	58	42	58.00	

FIG.17.4

Several tests of these wave patterns are described in the booklet "M and W Wave Patterns"(See App.J). The results of one of the tests is summarized in Fig.17.4 .

This test used a filter of 10%, and more than 2000 common stock waves were identified and classified.

To determine whether the period following each pattern had a bullish or a bearish bias, the pattern immediately following was noted. In other words, the patterns were considered in pairs, joined by a common turning point. The left hand pattern is the forecasting pattern, the right hand pattern described behavior following the forecasting pattern. The right hand pattern was called a bullish period if its far right turning point was higher than the first or left hand turning point. If the far right hand point was lower, it was rated a bearish period. For example, M1 is a bearish period; M10 is a bullish period.

It was then a simple counting problem for the computer. It was asked to count the number of bullish and the number of bearish periods following each pattern.

The performance in the test period is summarized by Fig.17.4. For example, the M1 wave was found 57 times. On 24 of the occasions, the next pattern was a rising period; on 33 occasions it was a declining period. The bullets mark significance above the 95.0% confidence level.

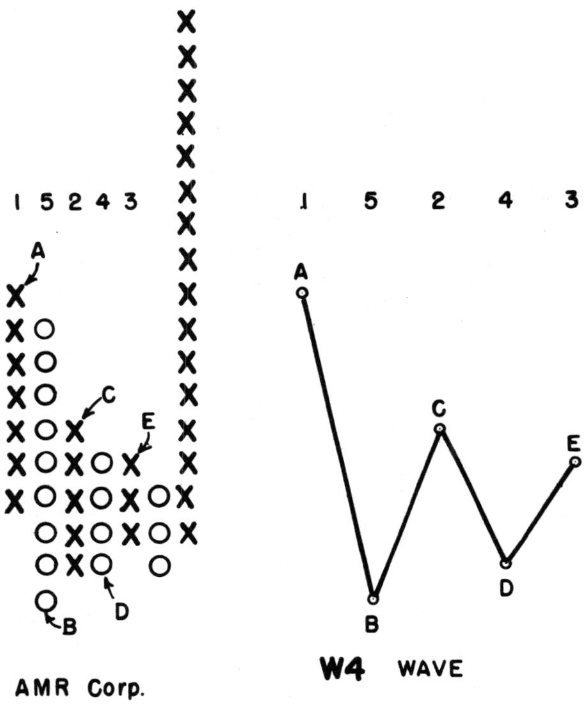

FIG.17.5

Point and Figure charts can be classified definitely if they are translated into MW waves. Note Fig.17.5 . The left hand chart is AMR Corp.(Source: Chartcraft) Note the three high turning points A,C,E and the two low turning points B,D. At the right these points are charted without the intermediate X and O columns. A is the highest rank, C is second highest; on down to the lowest B which is rank 5. This gives the identification number 15243 which is a W4 wave. In table Fig.17.4 you will see that this wave, a triangle, was found 33 times; 26 times it was followed by a rising wave; 7 times by a declining wave. It evidently has a bullish bias, which was acknowledged in the P and F chart (Fig.17.5) by a fine rising column of Xs.

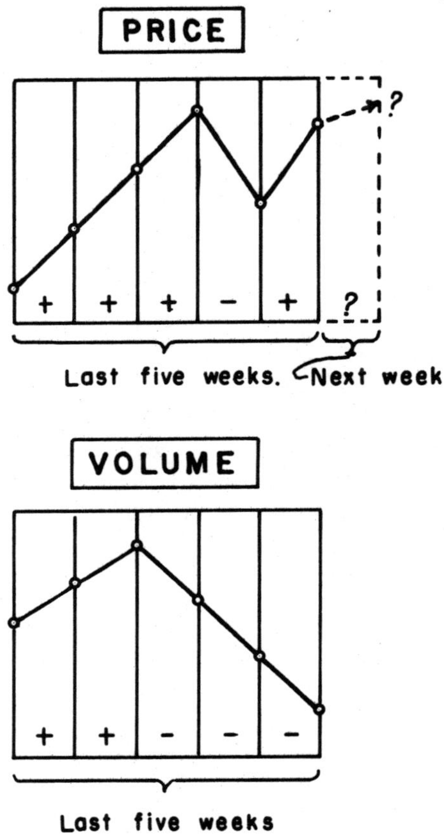

FIG.18.1

18. BEHAVIOR IN TIME PATTERNS:

Suppose that amounts of change are ignored, and that we consider only the direction of change in a time pattern.

Note Fig.18.1. Suppose that prices, in the last five weeks, rose in the first three weeks, then declined, then rose again in the last week.. This could be symbolized + + + - +.

Suppose that, in the same five weeks, the volume of trading rose in the first two weeks, then declined in the following three weeks. This could be symbolized + + - - -.

How often has this wave pattern occurred in the past? What happened in the week following the pattern? How often did it rise in that week? How often did it decline? Is the difference sufficient to conclude that the wave has a bullish or a bearish bias?

It's important to note that the pattern is definitely defined. It can be positively identified, with no argument. The same is true with the MW waves in the preceding chapter. The result is that a computer can take over, examine the record, and report the behavior of the market following each pattern.

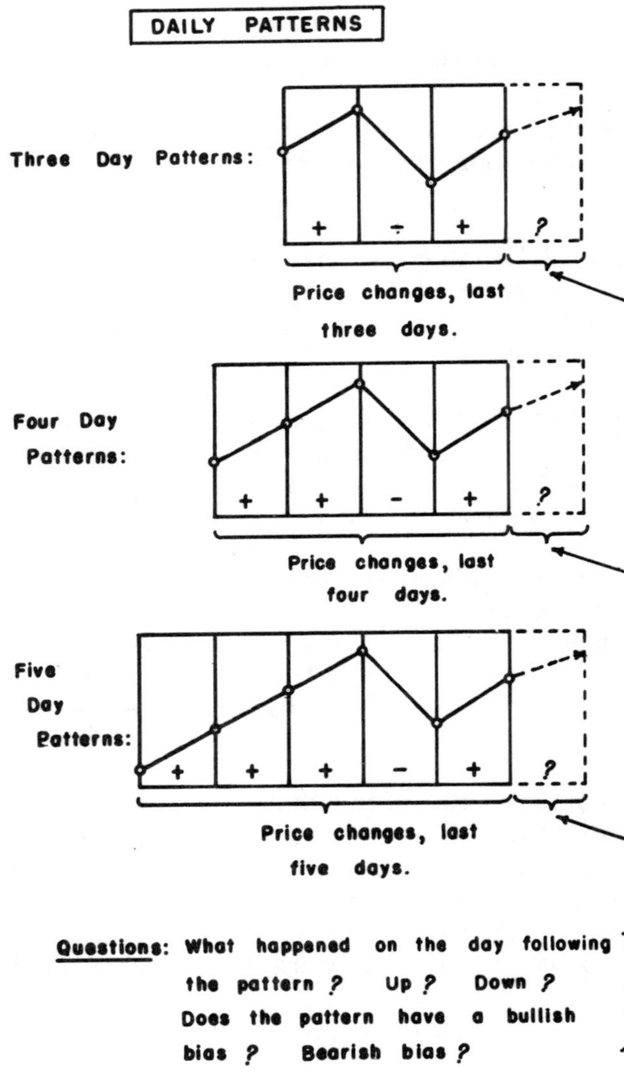
DAILY PATTERNS
Three Day Patterns:
+
÷
+
?
Price changes, last three days.
Four Day Patterns:
+
+
-
+
?
Price changes, last four days.
Five Day Patterns:
+
+
+
-
+
?
Price changes, last five days.
Questions: What happened on the day following the pattern ? Up ? Down ?
Does the pattern have a bullish bias ? Bearish bias ?

FIG.18.2

The time period can have several specific definitions, and each one can be tested. The pattern can be five days, four days , three days; it could be three hours, four hours, five hours. It could cover a span of three, four, or five weeks. See Fig.18.2.

Possible patterns for three time periods (days or weeks):

No.	Price:	Volume:	No.	Price:	Volume:
1	+++	+++	33	-++	+++
2	+++	++-	34	-++	++-
3	+++	+-+	35	-++	+-+
4	+++	+--	36	-++	+--
5	+++	-++	37	-++	-++
6	+++	-+-	38	-++	-+-
7	+++	--+	39	-++	--+
8	+++	---	40	-++	---
9	++-	+++	41	-+-	+++
10	++-	++-	42	-+-	++-
11	++-	+-+	43	-+-	+-+
12	++-	--	44	-+-	+--
13	++-	-++	45	-+-	-++
14	++-	-+-	46	-+-	-+-
15	++-	--+	47	-+-	--+
16	++-	---	48	-+-	---
17	+-+	+++	49	--+	+++
18	+-+	++-	50	--+	++-
19	+-+	+-+	51	--+	+-+
20	+-+	+--	52	--+	+--
21	+-+	-++	53	--+	-++
22	+-+	-+-	54	--+	-+-
23	+-+	--+	55	--+	--+
24	+-+	---	56	--+	---
25	+--	+++	57	---	+++
26	+--	++-	58	---	++-
27	+--	+-+	59	---	+-+
28	+--	+--	60	---	+--
29	+--	-++	61	---	-++
30	+--	-+-	62	---	-+-
31	+--	--+	63	---	--+
32	+--	---	64	---	---

FIG.18.3

For example, see Fig.18.3 .This figure lists all of the possible three day patterns of prices and volume. A computer check shows the following score for the most bullish and most bearish patterns, found from an examination of the D.J.Industrials every day in 28 years:

Most successful bullish three day patterns:

No.	percent	CS	
56	65.3	12.9	Highly significant
20	65.6	9.0	Significant
39	63.3	8.8	Significant
19	63.1	7.5	Significant
18	67.1	6.1	Probably significant
24	68.3	6.0	Probably significant

Most successful bearish three day patterns:

No.	percent	CS	
64	38.0	11.9	Highly significant
13	33.3	11.0	Highly significant
16	32.9	9.9	Significant
48	33.9	6.6	Probably significant
45	40.4	4.6	Probably significant
27	42.2	4.5	Probably significant

column heads in the above tables:

No.:See Fig.18.1 for pattern

Percent:Percent of the time the following day was a rising day.

CS: Chi squared, one degree of freedom, with Yates correction: this is a measure of significance.

(For a report on two, three, four, and five day, and two, three, four and five week patterns, see "Bias in Daily and Weekly Wave Patterns"; see App.J)

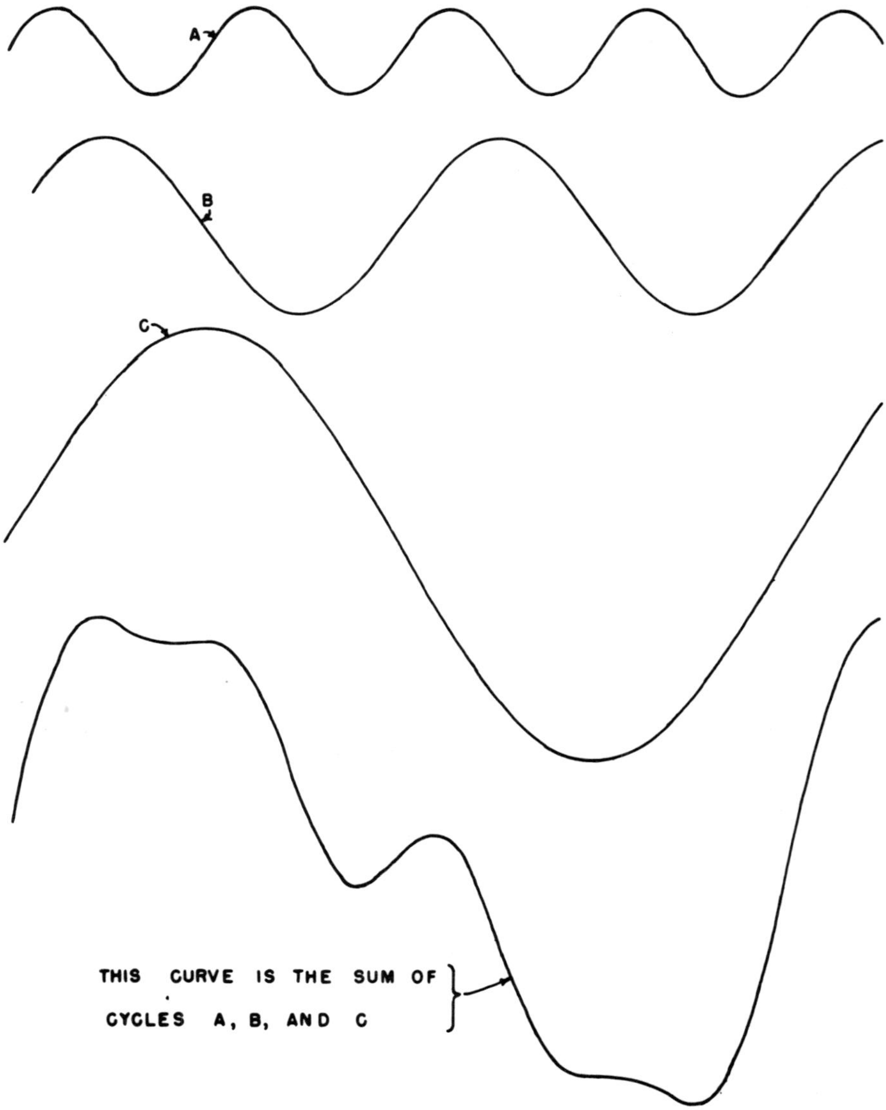

FIG.19.1

19. BEHAVIOR IN CYCLES:

Market behavior is characterized by waves and not by straight lines. Is there any underlying regularity?

The early chapters of this book reported on regular waves that are generated by the calendar.

In addition, mathematical analysis has been made practical by the development of the computer. It is possible to approximate any irregular curve by the addition of a number of regular sine waves. These can be calculated, and, if extrapolated into the future can produce a forecast expectation. Note Fig.19.1 .

An authority on cycle calculation, Gertrude Shirk of the Foundation for the Study of Cycles(A), reports that the most important underlying stock price cycles, ranked by amplitude at the crest, have been found to be the following:

Cycle:	Ideal Amplitude	Date of Phase: Current	Next:
46.2 years	32.0%	1965. crest	1988. trough
9.23 years	14.3%	1980.3 trough	1984.9 crest
15.37 years	13.5%	1982.0 trough	1989.7 crest
18.2 years	11.9%	1979.9 crest	1989.0 trough
5.01 years	6.5%	1983.4 trough	1985.9 crest
5.94 years	6.0%	1983.2 crest	1986.2 trough
4.80 years	5.0%	1983.2 crest	1985.6 trough

All of these cycles, with the exception of the 46 year cycle, have shown significance in statistical tests.

(A) For further study, see books and journals of The Foundation for the Study of Cycles,124 South Highland Ave.,Pittsburgh PA 15206

THE FIVE PERCENT PENETRATION METHOD

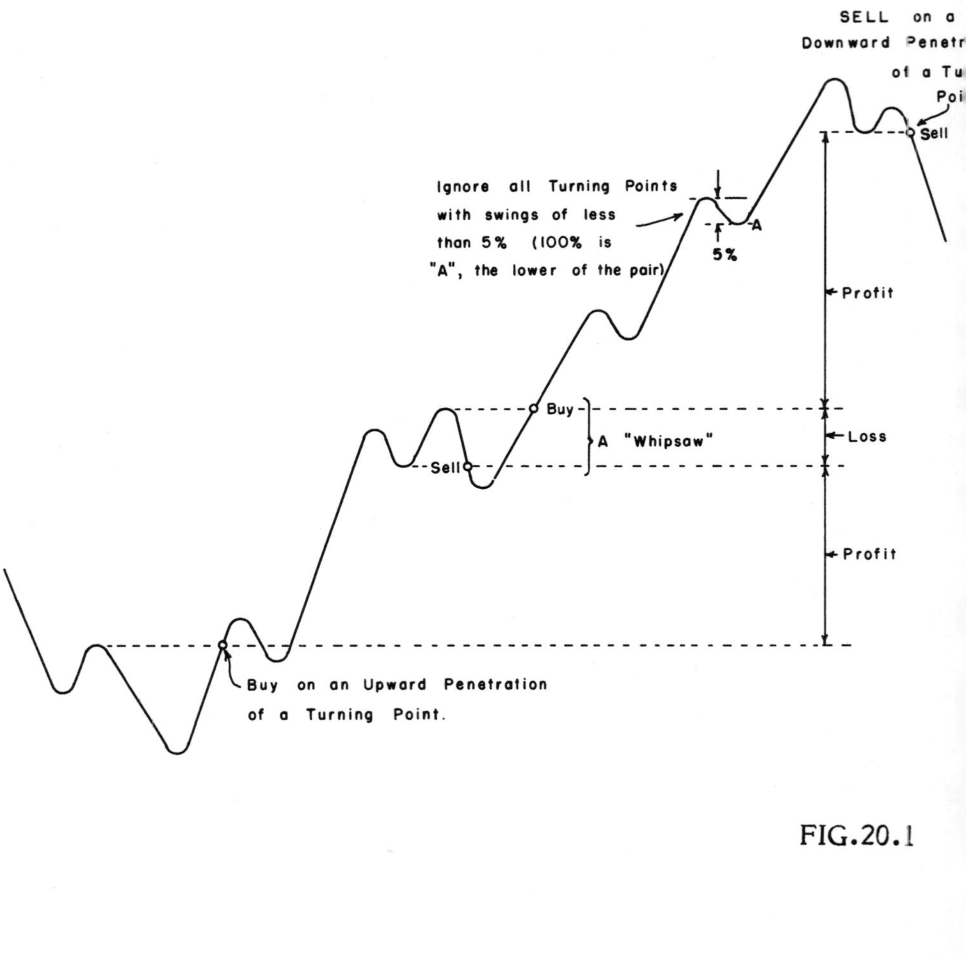

FIG.20.1

20.BEHAVIOR IN TRENDS

Dow's Theory for the determination of trend can be put into numbers by the simple device of ignoring, or filtering out, all swings below a specified level. The result of the Dow trend following technique can then be definitely tested.

Note Fig.20.1 . After filtering, breaks through the remaining turning points can be used as signals to buy or sell, and the success can be tested. The five percent definition was tested with the DJ Industrials over a 43 year time period (1897-1939). Buy and hold averaged 3.5% per year; the 5% filter averaged 12.3%. This wasn't adjusted for commission costs, so the actual improvement would be less.

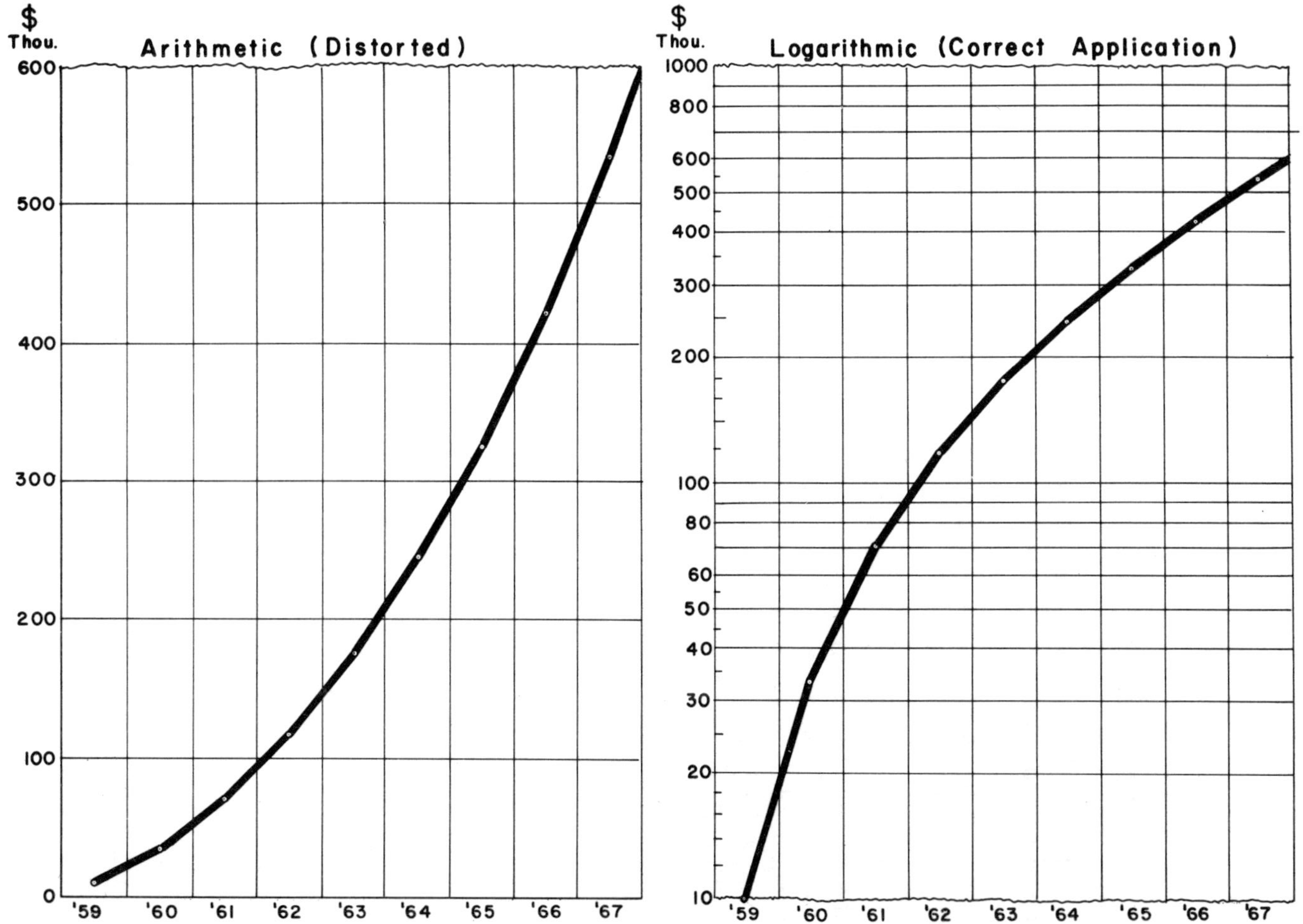
$ Thou.
Arithmetic (Distorted)
600
500
400
300
200
100
0
'59
'60
'61
'62
'63
'64
'65
'66
'67
$ Thou.
Logarithmic (Correct Application)
1000
800
600
500
400
300
200
100
80
60
50
40
30
20
10
'59
'60
'61
'62
'63
'64
'65
'66
'67

FIG.20.2

Another matter should be mentioned in this chapter on trends. Stock prices are sometimes charted on an arithmetic grid, with uniform spacing. Sometimes they are charted on a logarithmic grid, where equal percentage changes are given the same space. The latter, of course, is more correct; a one dollar change on a ten dollar stock is more important than a one dollar change on a hundred dollar stock. This is recognized on a logarithmic grid; on an arithmetic grid the changes appear to be the same.

For this reason, trend lines on an arithmetic grid are suspect; they can be deceptive. Note Fig.20.2 . Here exactly the same data has been charted on an arithmetic and on a logarithmic grid. The arithmetic chart is euphoric. The logarithmic grid gives the correct story; growth has been decelerating.

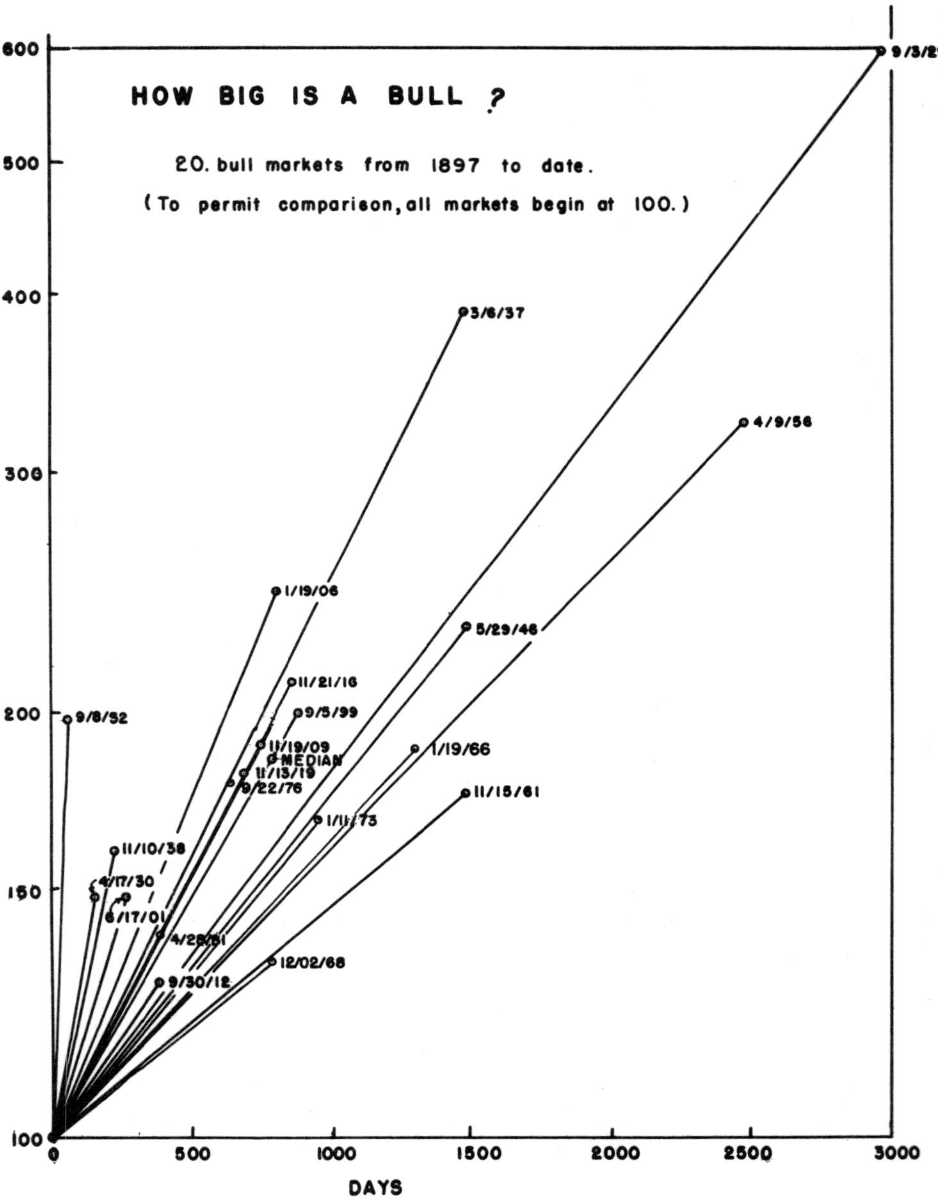

HOW BIG IS A BULL ?
20. bull markets from 1897 to date.
(To permit comparison, all markets begin at 100.)
600
500
400
300
200
150
100
0
500
1000
1500
2000
2500
3000
DAYS
9/3/29
3/6/37
4/9/56
1/19/06
5/29/46
11/21/16
9/5/99
9/8/32
11/19/09
MEDIAN
11/13/19
9/22/76
1/19/66
11/15/61
1/11/73
11/10/38
4/17/30
6/17/01
4/28/61
12/02/68
9/30/12

FIG.21.1

21. BEHAVIOR IN BULL AND BEAR MARKETS

The stock market is never stable. The big swings up or down are called bull and bear markets; lesser swings are called secondary reactions in bull markets and rallies in bear markets.

Since swings come in assorted sizes, how can we differentiate a rally from a full bull market? When does a reaction become big enough to be called a bear market?

After consulting the stock market histories, we find that a filter of 30% works quite well. Swings of larger than 30% include all of the accepted bull and bear markets and a few that are marginal.

Figure 21.1 compares the magnitude and age of the twenty bull markets since 1897. The median is a 95% rise and age of 28 months. Figure 21.2 charts the twenty bear markets. Since the 30% filter is calculated from the low point, a decline of 23% is the equivalent of a 30% swing. The median bear has a decline of 37% and an age of 18 months.

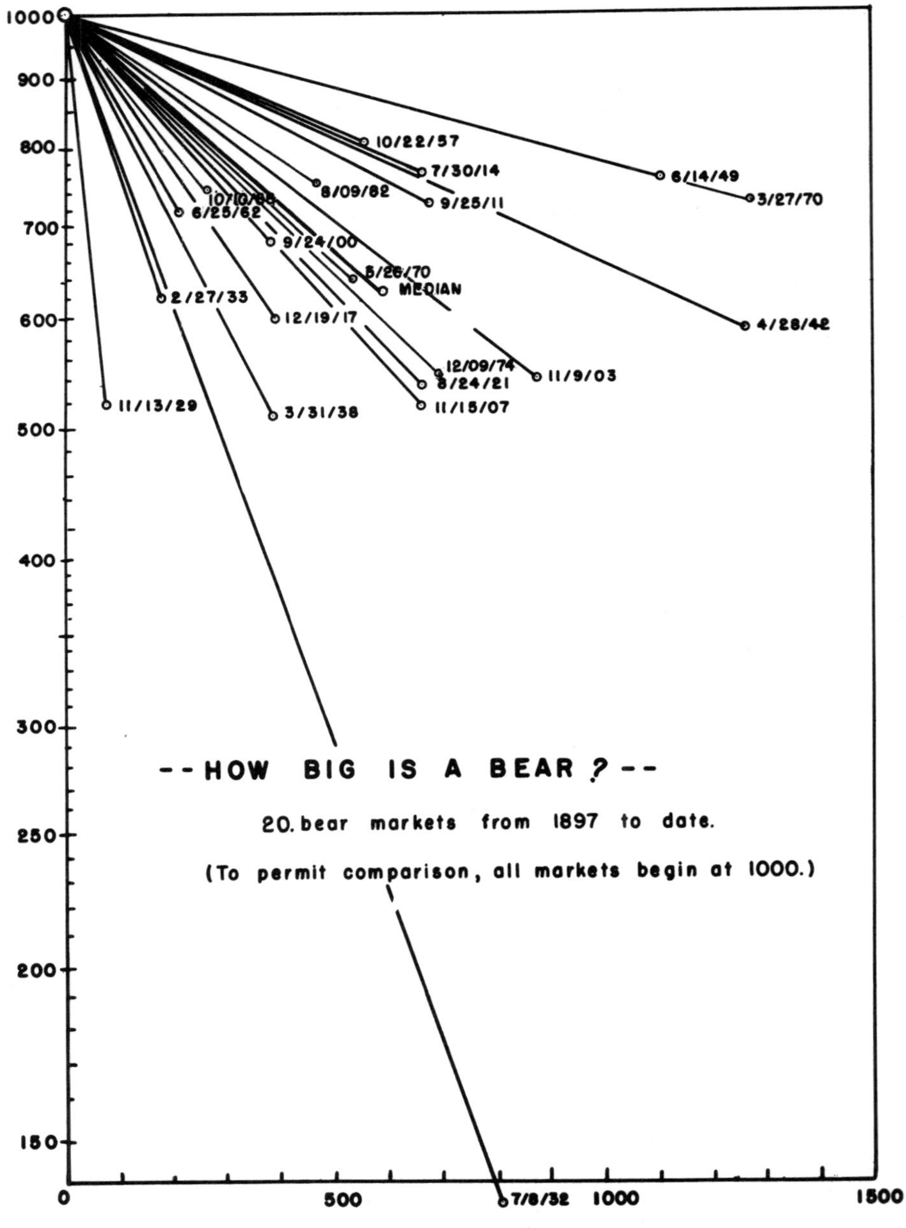

1000
900
800
700
600
500
400
300
250
200
150
0
500
1000
1500
DAYS
10/22/57
7/30/14
6/14/49
3/27/70
8/09/82
9/25/11
10/10/66
6/25/62
9/24/00
5/26/70
MEDIAN
2/27/33
12/19/17
4/28/42
12/09/74
8/24/21
11/9/03
11/13/29
3/31/38
11/15/07
7/8/32
--HOW BIG IS A BEAR?--
20. bear markets from 1897 to date.
(To permit comparison, all markets begin at 1000.)

FIG.21.2

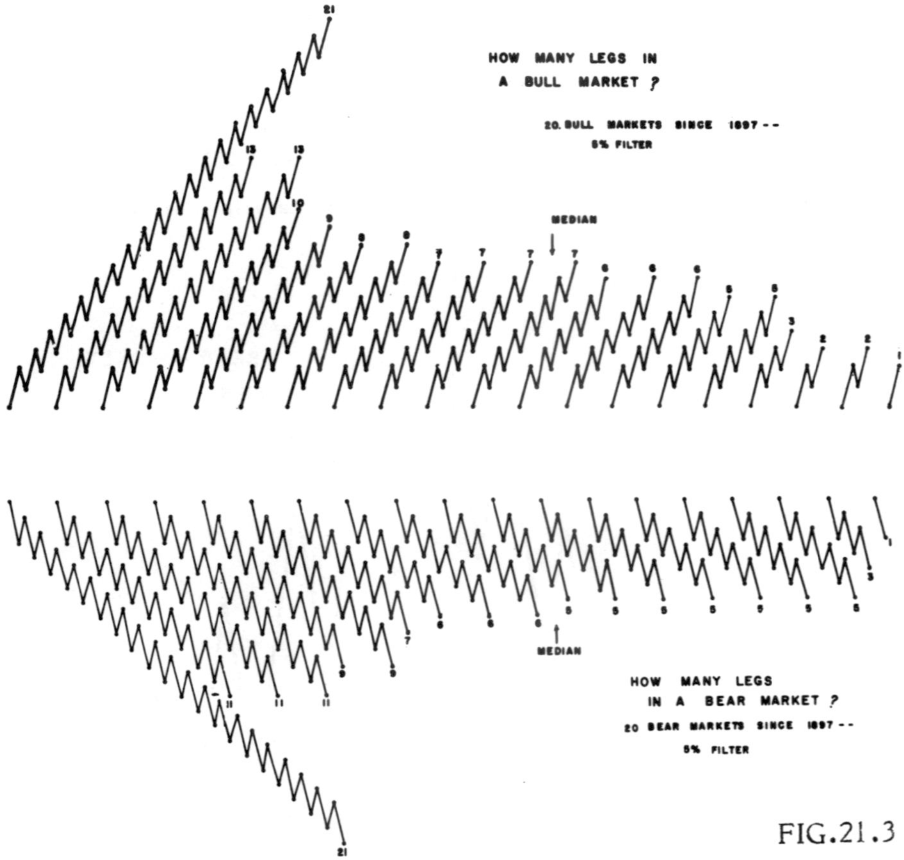

FIG.21.3

When does a decline move from the minor league and qualify to be called a secondary reaction? When does an upswing deserve to be called a rally? There is no fixed definition. We've found that a filter of 10% results in an average of two reactions in a bull market, which is the Elliott wave count. However, it gives an average of three rallies in a bear market.

If the filter is set lower, the number of rallies and reactions increase. Figure 21.3 charts the number of rallies and reactions if the filter is 5%. This is a good sized swing; it's fifty points when the Dow is at 1000.

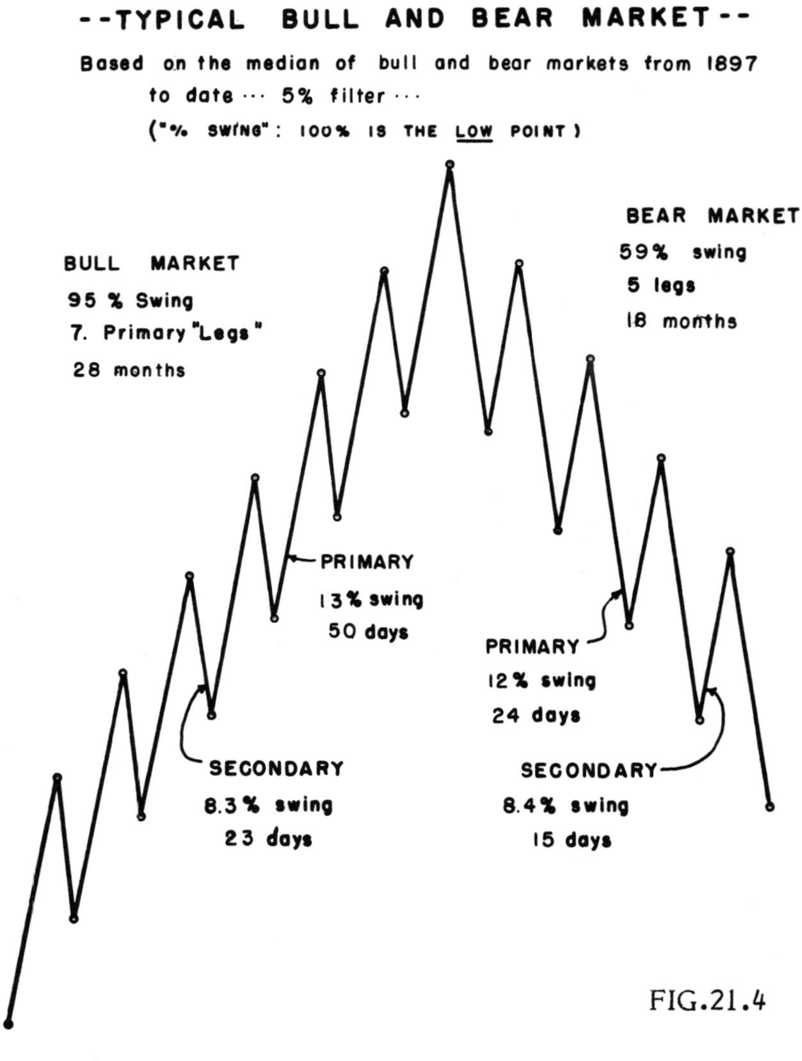

FIG.21.4

Figure 21.4 charts the average bull and bear market, if a filter of 30% is used to define the bull and bear markets, and a 5% filter is used to qualify as a secondary or a rally.

For more details, see "Filtered Waves, Basic Theory" (App.J).

21. CONCLUSIONS:

The conclusion of this book is that the market has definite upward tendencies at certain predictable times; it was leanings in the downward direction at other predictable times.

These inclinations and biases should be useful both to speculators and to investors. If a purchase is being considered, and the market has a downward bias, a prudent man should delay purchase. If the bias is upward, purchase should be made immediately. On the other hand, if a sale is contemplated, and the market has a downward bias, a prudent man should sell immediately.

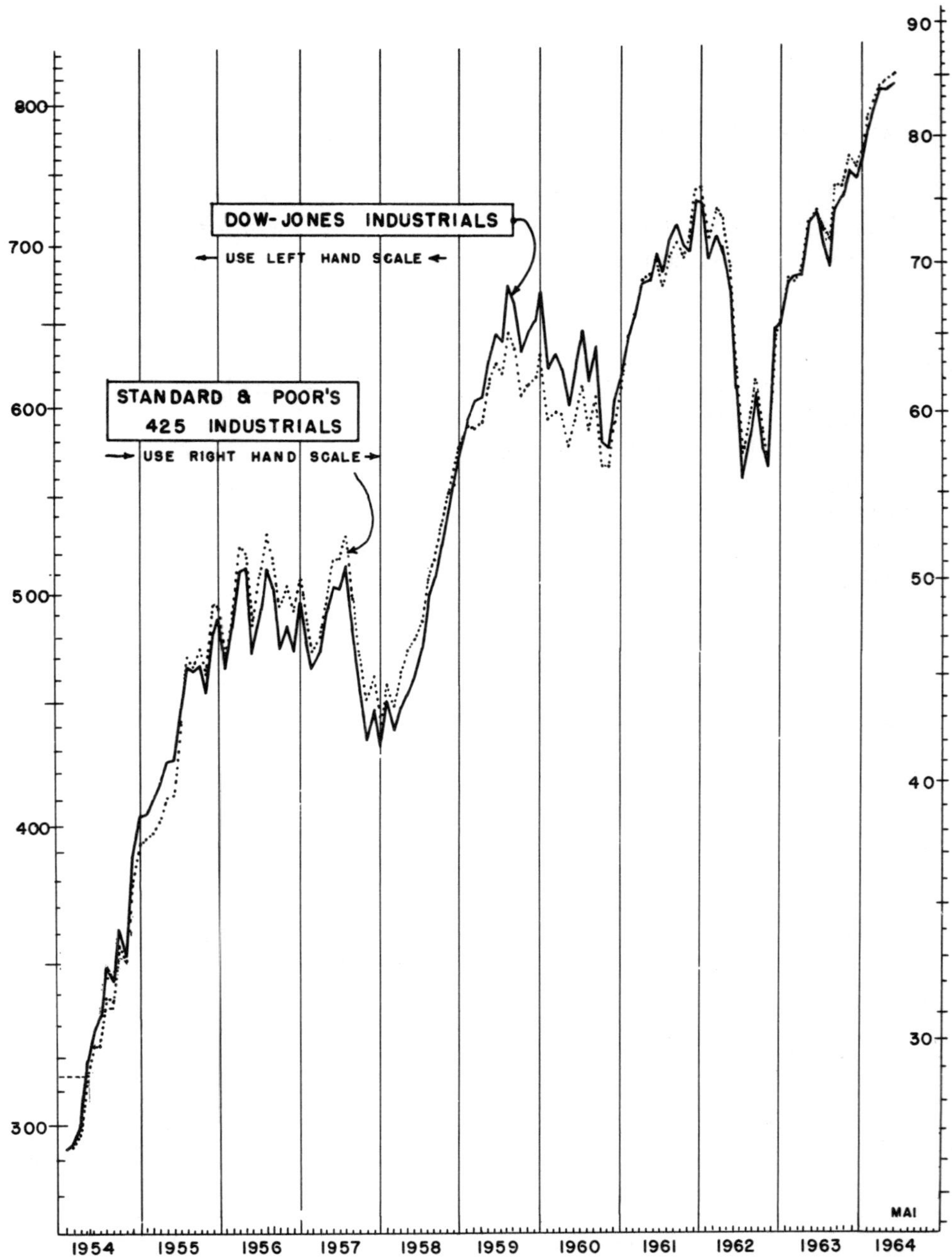

DOW-JONES INDUSTRIALS
USE LEFT HAND SCALE
STANDARD & POOR'S 425 INDUSTRIALS
USE RIGHT HAND SCALE
800
700
600
500
400
300
90
80
70
60
50
40
30
MAI
1954
1955
1956
1957
1958
1959
1960
1961
1962
1963
1964

FIG.A1

Appendix A.

ARE THE DJ INDUSTRIALS REPRESENTATIVE?

Most of the work in this book has been derived from the behavior of the DJ Industrial average. Is this index representative? It's based on only 30 blue chip stocks, and ignores the stocks of small companies.

In 1896, Charles Dow began to report the averages of a few selected industrial stocks. After 88 years of use, it is still the most widely quoted measure, although a number of very sophisticated indexes have entered the field.

Twelve industrial stocks were used until 1916, when the list was increased to 20, and the new average was worked back to December 1914. Only the closing averages were calculated. The method was simple. The stock prices were listed and totaled, then divided by the number of stocks to get an average. If a stock split, a multiple was applied before adding with the others; if the split was two-for-one, for example, the stock price after the split was always multiplied by two before combining with the other prices.

On October 1, 1928, a number of changes were made. The number of Industrial stocks was increased to 30; the closing prices were supplemented by highs and lows for the day; the method of coping with splits was altered. The multiples were eliminated, and the adjustment was made by a final divisor. The divisor was adjusted when a new stock was substituted for another in the list, in order to give continuity.

To calculate the current average, list the stocks (you will find the list occasionally in Barron's and the Wall Street Journal.) Set down the prices; add them up; divide by the divisor (see Barron's or the Wall Street Journal); the result is the index.

The index has limitations:

1.Representation. The index is based on the stock prices of thirty large companies. It is an important list. If you will multiply the price of each stock by the number of shares issued, you will find that this small group of stocks has more than 20% of the value of all stocks on the New York Exchange. Small stocks aren't included, but note Fig.A1. This chart compares the Dow Industrials with the all-inclusive New York Stock Exchange index. I think you will agree that the Dow seems to do a good job.

The New York Stock Exchange index weights the stocks by their capitalization. But doesn't this make sense? A recent report shows that General Electric is held by more than a thousand institutional portfolios. General Nutrition is held by less than twenty. Certainly General Electric is more important,should be given more weight in the index.

2.Price level. A minor irritation is the high price of the Dow Jones Industrials. A change of ten points appears important; actually it's only 1% of 1000.

3.A more serious objection is levelled at the high-low calculation. These are not true highs and lows for the index. Instead , they are calculated from the highs and lows of the individual stocks. Since these highs and lows occur at different times in the day, the average is never as high as the published "high"; it never drops down to the "low".

4.Weighting: Statisticians wince when they learn the weighting method. In a representative average, each component should be weighted by its importance. In the Dow the stocks are weighted by their prices. For example, Exxon has five times the capitalization of Merck, and should carry more weight. However, because of the high price per share of Merck , it carries twice the weight and is twice as important in the index as Exxon.

The lack of logic in the weighting method becomes evident at the time of a split. If a Dow stock is split four-for-one, for example, its influence in the index is reduced by 75%. Price changes in the stock will now influence the overall average by one quarter of the former effect.

It should be noted that lower priced stocks are usually more volatile; this reduces the effect of the lower weight given to low priced stocks.

Conclusion? The average has many limitations, but, as noted in Fig.A1, it manages to do a good job.

Appendix B.

EVALUATION OF TURNING POINTS:

The analysis of waves and patterns in the market can be made definite by a simple device: Select a percentage for the size of a wave that will be recognized; ignore or "filter out" all of the smaller moves.

This simple device permits the classification of a turning point as valid or invalid in the Dow Theory.

If you are familiar with the point and figure method of charting, you will notice a similarity. Point and Figure uses a definite number of points to recognize a turning point; wave filters use a definite percentage.

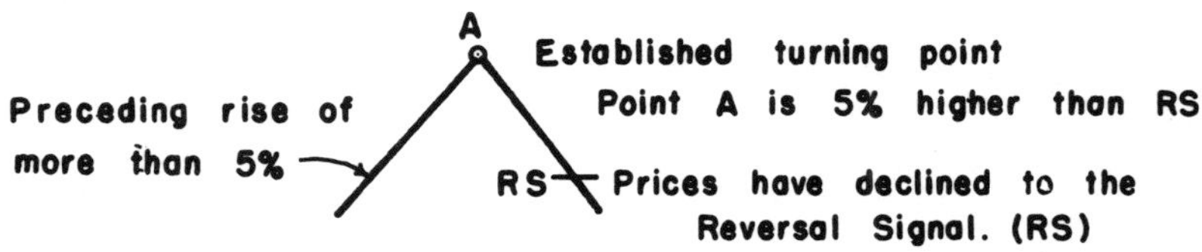

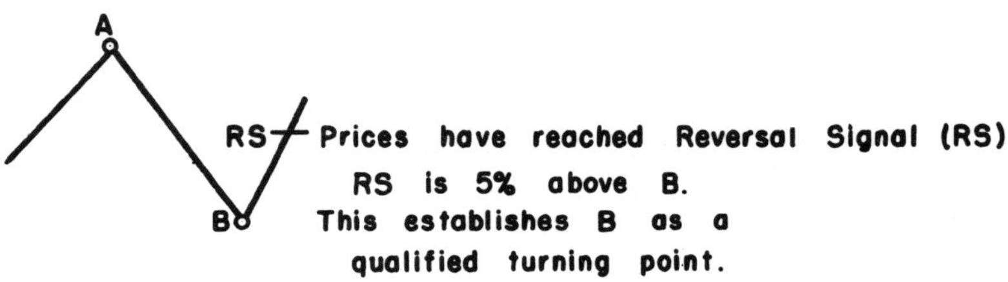

FIG.B1

For an example of the use of the percentage filter, see Fig.B1. A 5% filter has been specified. The upper point A is recognized as a valid turning point when prices have retreated to RS, which is 5% below A. Point B is recognized as valid when prices have reversed 5% to RS in the lower chart.

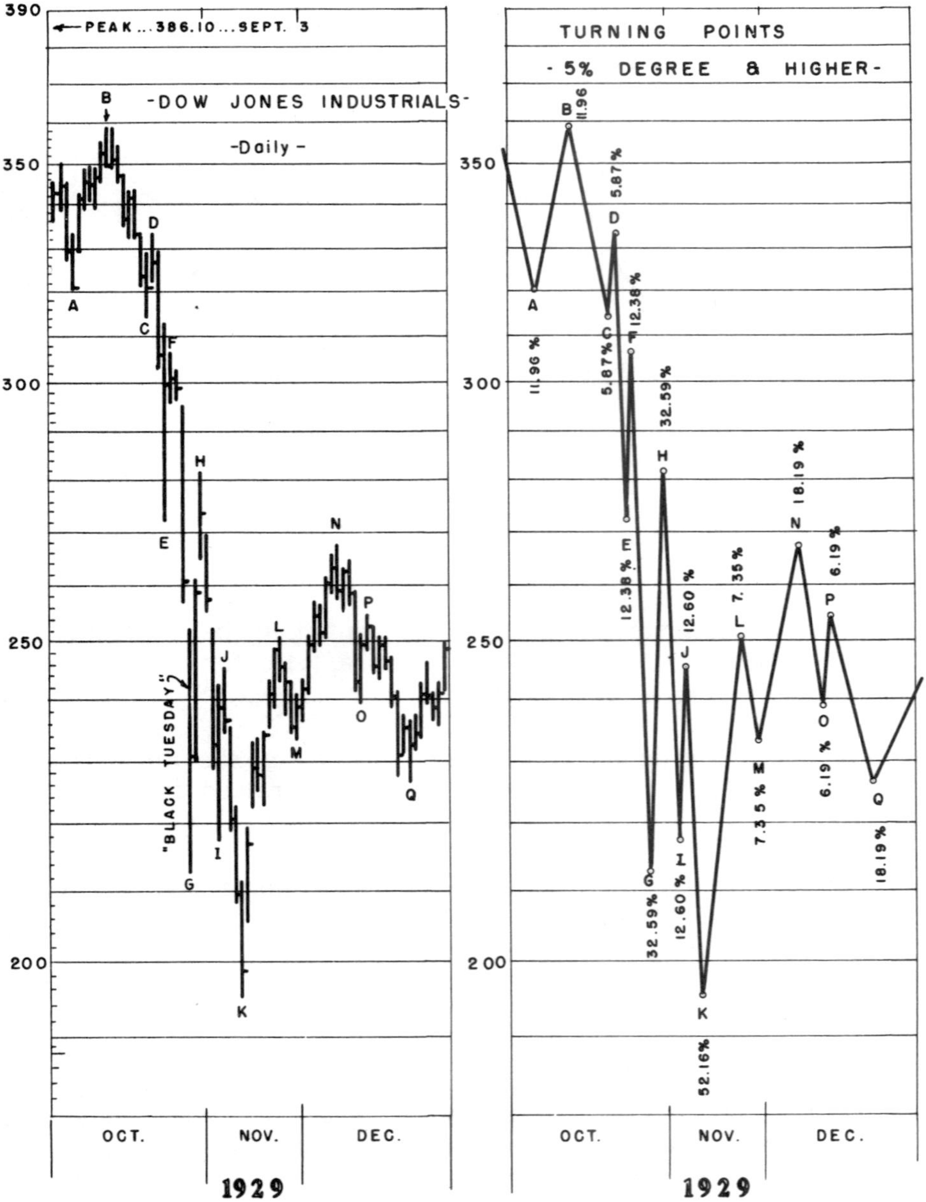

FIG.B2

For an example of application, note the year 1929 in Fig. B2.

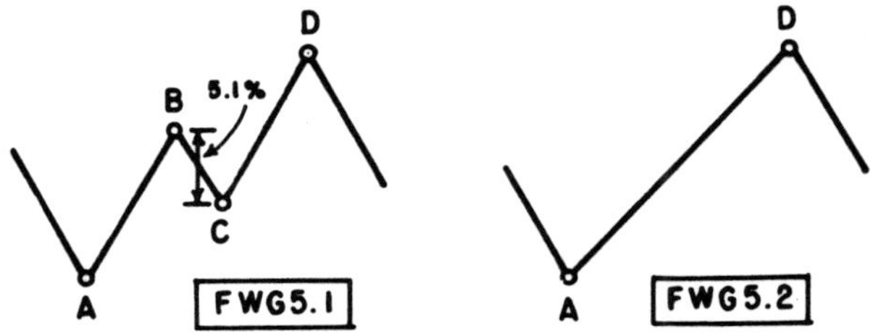

FIG.B3

The importance of a turning point can be measured. Note Fig.B3. The left hand chart uses a 5.1% filter; the one at the right uses a 5.2% filter.

Note the turning points B and C. Now you see them; now you don't. They vanish when the filter is raised from 5.1% to 5.2%.

This provides a simple method for the evaluation of turning points. Their importance can be measured by the filter required to eliminate them.

To apply this method, turning points must be identified in pairs . To qualify for measurement, there are two requirements: The swing preceding the pair must be larger (A must be below C.) and the following swing must be larger (D must be above B). When a pair qualifies, the turning points can be evaluated by taking the percentage difference.

The example in Fig.B3 measures a reaction in a rising trend. Exactly the same method, in mirror image, can be used for the evaluation of a rally in a downtrend. Note points O and P in the 1929 chart (Fig.B2).

Appendix C.

WHAT IS THE DOW THEORY?

The Dow Theory began with Charles Dow (1850-1902), founder of the Dow Jones News Service, and founder and first editor of the Wall Street Journal. In his capacity, he wrote many editorials on the subject of the market. These editorials are the foundations of the Dow Theory. His work has endured. Today the interpretation of his ideas is providing a livelihood for many men.

S.A.Nelson, a writer and publisher, tried to persuade Dow to write a book summarizing his ideas, but didn't succeed. Nelson had determination, however, and collected all of the important editorials from the files of the Wall Street Journal . He published these in a small book "The ABC of Stock Speculation." (App.J) In this book he labelled the Dow chapters "Dow's Theory", and the name was established.

A few years after Dow's death, William Peter Hamilton became editor of the Wall Street Journal. He proceeded to develop Dow's ideas from the status of general statements into a workable method. In 1922 he wrote a book "The Stock Market Barometer" (App.J) , which erected a structure on Dow's foundation. A short time before his death he supported his thesis by a famous editorial "The Turn of the Tide." This editorial, in the October 23, 1929 Wall Street Journal (one week before Black Tuesday) definitely called the end of the long bull market and the beginning of the great bear market.

Robert Rhea (1887-1939), because of an airplane accident in the first world war, was bedridden from 1918 to his death. In Colorado Springs, he began a study of the Dow ideas -- first as a hobby, and later as a profitable vocation. His own wealth accelerated from the practice of his ideas. He was long of stocks through most of the twenties; he had no stocks at the time of the 1929 crash; he thereafter sold short for two years. I'm prejudiced in favor of Rhea's contributions, because he liked to count and measure.(This is the underlying thesis of the book you are reading.)

Another capable interpreter was E.George Schaefer, author of "How I Helped More than 10,000 investors to Profit in Stocks." (App.J) In this book he developed his ideas of a "New Dow Theory." Schaefer believed in investing with the primary trend, and didn't advocate selling on secondaries.

Some very capable students of the Dow Theory are active today. One of the best is Richard Russell of San Diego. Russell has written a book "The Dow Theory Today" (see App.J).

Many books have been written on the Theory, but the fundamentals are not complicated. Hamilton wrote "The essence of Dow's Theory can be summed up in three sentences. In an editorial December 19,1900, he says 'The market is always to be considered as having three movements, all going on at the same time. The first is the narrow movement from day to day. The second is the short swing, running from two weeks to a month or more; the third is the main movement , covering at least four years in its duration.'"

Hamilton's quotation was an oversimplification, of course. Actually , it is an example of the beginnings of the "Theory." The outline which follows is a condensation of writings on the subject.

THE DOW THEORY: A SEVEN POINT SUMMARY:

(1) The fluctuations of the Dow Jones rail and industrial averages are a composite index of all the hopes, fears, and knowledge of everyone who knows anything of financial matters. They therefore can serve as a barometer of the future. Hamilton wrote "Consciously or unconsciously the movements of prices reflect not the past but the future. When coming events cast their shadows before, the shadows fall on the New York Stock Exchange."

Rhea believed that students should concentrate their studies on the averages - other statistics could be ignored!

(2) The market consists of three movements, which are going on at the same time:

(2A) The Primary Markets. These are the great bull and bear markets. They last from one year to several years. These great movements are fundamental in nature, and are beyond the reach of manipulation.

(2B) The Secondary Movements: These moves are called Primary Swings (or legs) when in the direction of the Primary Market. When in the other direction (rallies in bear markets, declines in bull markets) they are called Secondary Reactions. The Secondary Reactions are distinguished from minor changes by their magnitude (usually sufficient to retrace one-third to two-thirds of the preceding primary swing and by their duration (three weeks to three months)

(2C) The minor or day-to-day movements. If the Primary Movement is considered a tide, the secondary is similar to the waves that please the surfboard enthusiasts, and the minor movements are the small ripples. The minor movements are not considered important in the Dow Theory.

DOW THEORY - BASIC

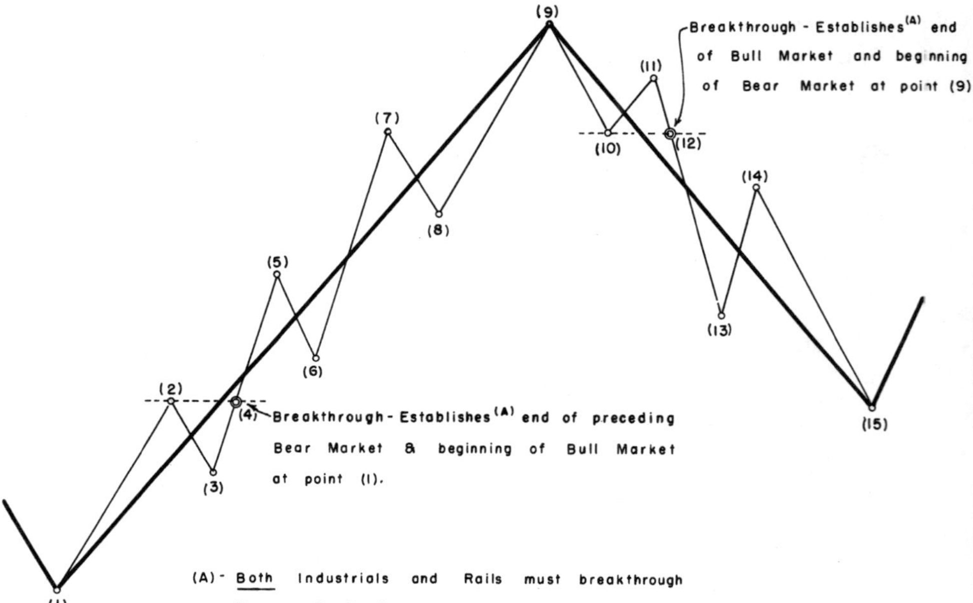

(A) - Both Industrials and Rails must breakthrough (i.e. confirm) for a valid signal.

PRIMARY MARKETS: (1)-(9) -- Bull Market
(9)-(15) -- Bear Market

These Primary Markets last from one year to several years.

PRIMARY SWINGS: (1)-(2), (3)-(5), (6)-(7), (8)-(9), (9)-(10), (11)-(13), (14)-(15)

(Also called "legs".)

SECONDARY REACTIONS: (2)-(3), (5)-(6), (7)-(8), (10)-(11), (13-14)

These last from three weeks to three months and retrace (i.e. "correct") 1/3 to 2/3 of the preceding Primary Swing.

FIG.C1

(3) The great bull and bear markets each consist of three phases. These are not related to the secondary movements described above in (2) and should be considered separately:

(3A) In a Bull Market, the First Phase represents the improvement in public confidence and a correction of the undervaluation developed in the last phase of the preceding bear market.

The Second Phase is a response to improvement in corporate earnings.

The Third Phase is one of rampant speculation, when stocks are advanced on "hopes and expectations."

(3B) In a Bear Market, the First Phase is a correction of the speculative excesses of the preceding Bull Market.

The Second Phase is a deterioration of prices in gear with a slide in the earnings of shares.

The Third Phase is a final depression of prices caused in part by distress selling.

(4) The trend can be determined by the action of the secondary swings. Refer to the chart. The rise from point (1) to (2) , at the time, might be considered a secondary reaction in the preceding bear market. But when prices turned upward at point (3), which is higher than (1), the picture begins to look bullish. Then, when prices broke through the level of (2) at point (4), the rise is known to be part of a bull market which began at point (1).

In a downward swing, the same type of analysis would be valid. In the drop from (9) to (10), the classification would be "secondary reaction" until the drop at point (11), when the classification becomes dubious. Then, at the breakthrough at point (12), the classification is definitely changed to "Bear Market."

This method of determining trends by "breakthrough" has been aptly compared to the determination of tides by the extent of waves on a sandy beach. If the farthest sweep of the wave is marked by a stick, and the next wave carries beyond this point (a breakthrough), the tide is probably rising.

(5) In determining the trend in (4), both Industrial and Rail averages must be considered. Breakthroughs by one average are not considered signals until the move is confirmed by the other average. The confirming action, however, need not be on the same day.

(6) The averages sometimes move horizontally, within a 5% band, for three weeks or longer. When both average do this, it's called a "Line." When both averages break out of this "Line" in the same direction, an important move in the same direction is probable. The breakout is usually made with an increase in volume.

Hamilton noted that "lines" seldom occur at the beginning or ending of secondary swings, but usually in the center.

Rhea's analysis recommends the consideration of "lines" of less than 5%. If both averages, for example, have been moving in a 2% band, a breakout from the band would be significant.

Rhea found that in a bull market, downside penetrations of "lines" are very speculative, while upside penetrations are more reliable.

(7) Volume: A market which is "overbought" becomes dull on rallies and develops activity on declines. Conversely, in "oversold" markets the tendency is to become dull on declines and active on rallies.

Robert Rhea supplemented Hamilton's tabulations with a detailed listing of all of the bull and bear markets and secondary movements in the period from 1896 to the time of his death in 1939. These tabulations have been charted in Fig.C2 and Fig.C3. The data follows in Fig.C4 and Fig.C5. The Primary Markets are traced with heavy lines; the light lines are the Secondary Movements. In addition, the points of confirmation of the primary markets are marked with the letter "C". Profits and losses obtained by buying and selling at these points of confirmation are indicated by arrows. Since the confirmation always follows the top or the bottom of a primary market, the profits are always less than the total move.

You can profit from this theory. It doesn't always give a correct forecast, and the forecast isn't always clear. But the profits over the years, when cumulated , are much better than "buy and hold".

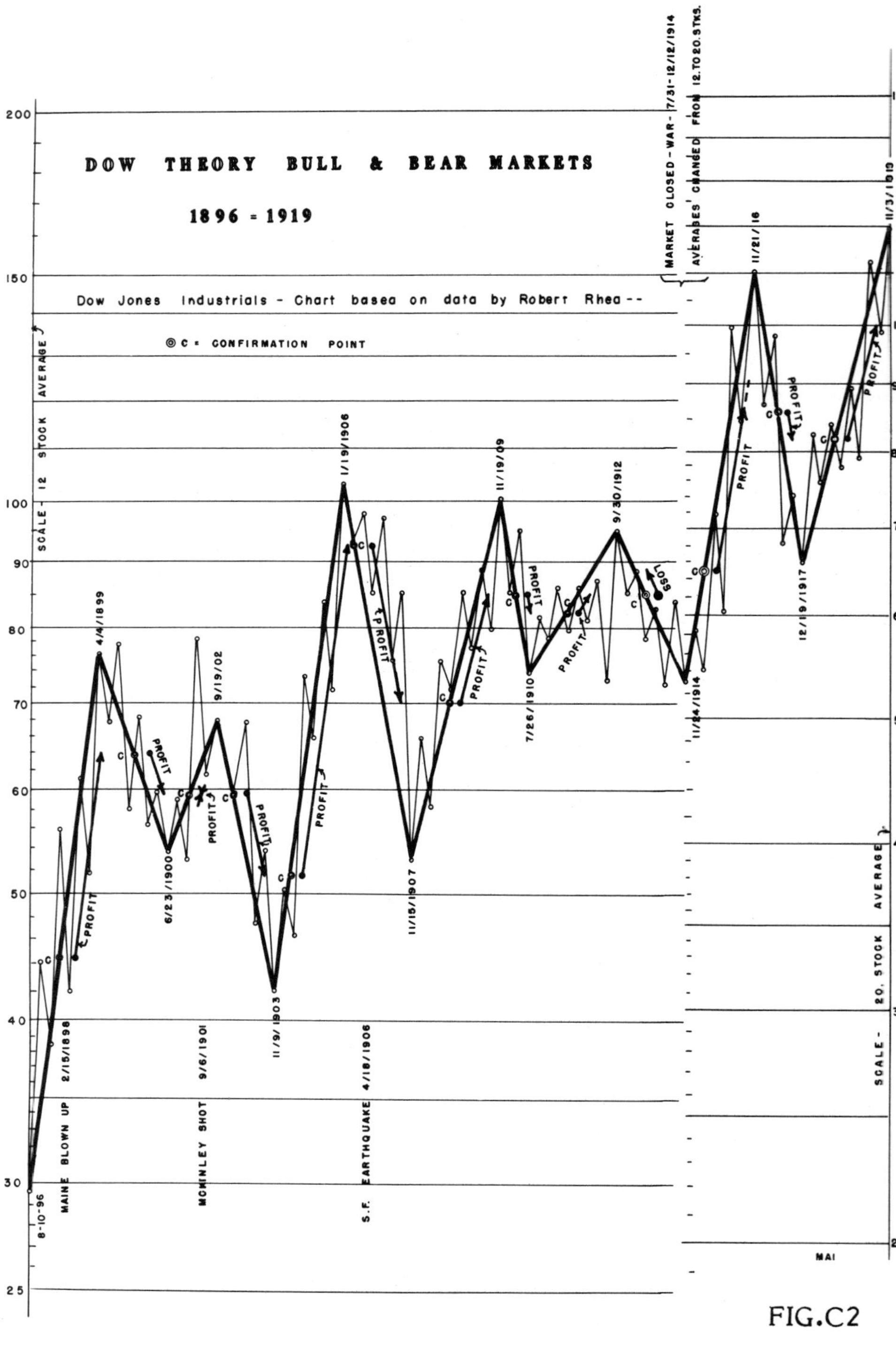
DOW THEORY BULL & BEAR MARKETS
1896 - 1919
Dow Jones Industrials - Chart based on data by Robert Rhea--
◎ C = CONFIRMATION POINT
SCALE - 12 STOCK AVERAGE
SCALE - 20. STOCK AVERAGE
MARKET CLOSED - WAR - 7/31 - 12/12/1914
AVERAGES CHANGED FROM 12. TO 20. STKS.
8-10-96
2/15/1898
MAINE BLOWN UP
4/4/1899
6/23/1900
9/6/1901
MCKINLEY SHOT
9/19/02
11/9/1903
1/19/1906
4/18/1906
S.F. EARTHQUAKE
11/15/1907
11/19/09
7/26/1910
9/30/1912
11/24/1914
11/21/16
12/19/1917
11/3/1919
PROFIT
LOSS
MAI

FIG.C2

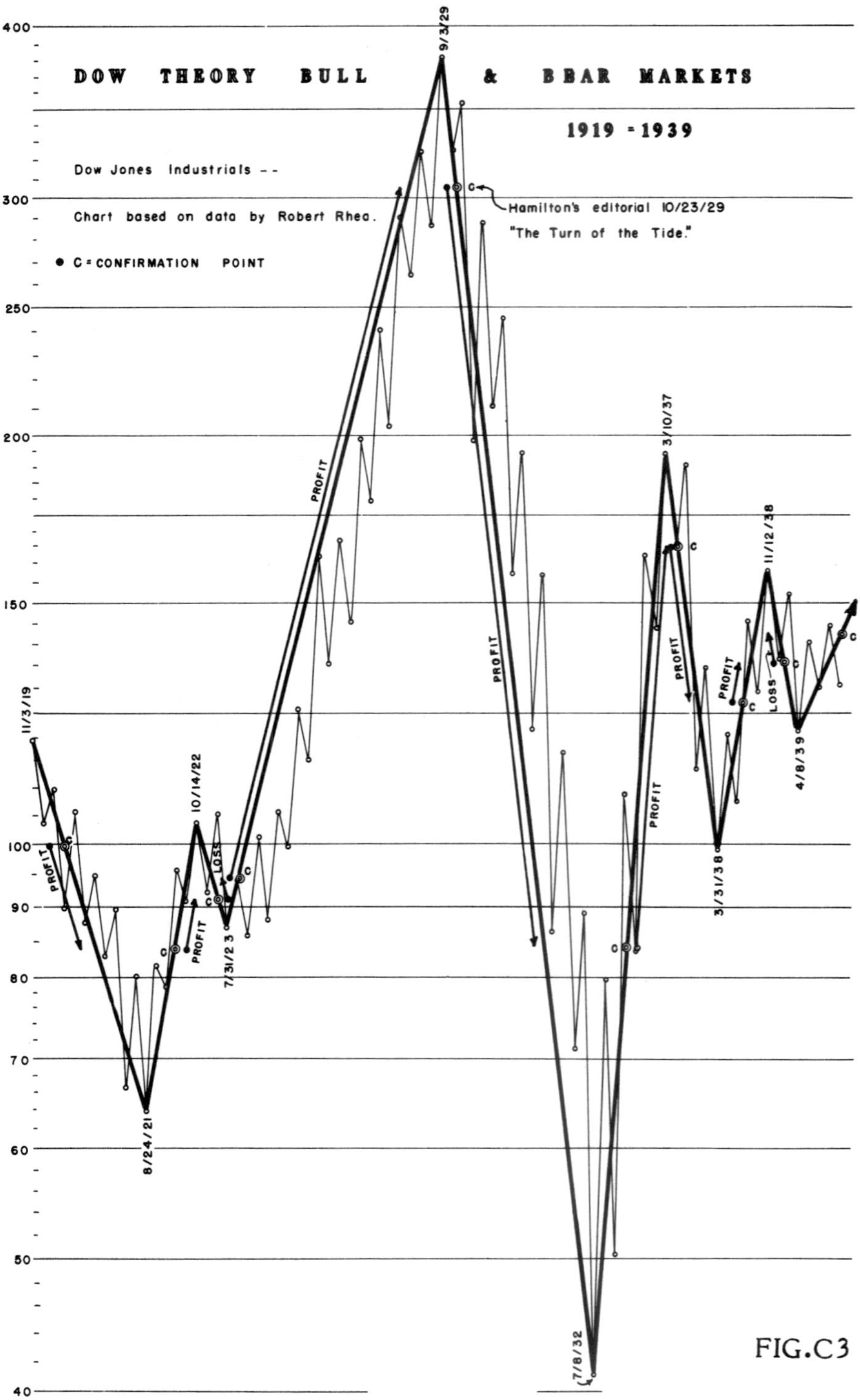

DOW THEORY BULL & BEAR MARKETS
1919 - 1939
Dow Jones Industrials --
Chart based on data by Robert Rhea.
● C = CONFIRMATION POINT
Hamilton's editorial 10/23/29
"The Turn of the Tide."
400
300
250
200
150
100
90
80
70
60
50
40
11/3/19
8/24/21
10/14/22
7/31/23
9/3/29
7/8/32
3/10/37
3/31/38
11/12/38
4/8/39
PROFIT
LOSS
C

FIG.C3

DOW THEORY - DATES OF PRIMARY AND SECONDARY MOVEMENTS - from Robert Rhea -
(Prices are D-J Industrial Closing Prices.)

Bull	8/10/96	29.64
	11/9/96	44.08
	4/19/97	38.49
	9/10/97	55.82
	3/25/98	42.00
	8/26/98	60.97
	10/19/98	51.56
Bear	4/4/99	76.04
	5/31/99	67.51
	9/5/99	77.61
	12/18/99	58.27
	2/5/00	68.36
	5/15/00	56.62
	6/1/00	59.38
Bull	6/23/00	53.68
	7/23/00	59.02
	9/24/00	52.96
	6/17/01	78.26
	12/14/01	61.52
Bear	9/19/02	67.77
	12/15/02	59.57
	2/16/03	67.70
	8/8/03	47.38
	8/17/03	53.88
Bull	11/9/03	42.15
	1/27/04	50.50
	3/12/04	46.41
	12/5/04	73.23
	12/12/04	65.77
	4/14/05	83.75
	5/22/05	71.37
Bear	1/19/06	103.00
	3/5/06	92.90
	4/3/06	98.19
	7/13/06	85.18
	10/9/06	96.75
	3/25/07	75.39
	5/3/07	85.02
Bull	11/15/07	53.00
	1/14/08	65.84
	2/13/08	58.62
	5/18/08	75.12
	6/23/08	71.70
	8/10/08	85.40
	9/22/08	77.07
	11/13/08	88.38
	2/23/09	79.91
	11/19/09	100.53

Bear	11/19/09	100.53
	2/8/10	85.03
	3/8/10	94.56
Bull	7/26/10	73.62
	8/17/10	81.41
	9/6/10	78.35
	10/18/10	86.02
	12/6/10	79.68
	2/4/11	86.02
	4/22/11	81.32
	6/19/11	87.06
	9/25/11	72.94
Bear	9/30/12.	94.15
	12/11/12	85.25
	1/9/13	88.57
	3/20/13	78.25
	4/4/13	83.19
	6/11/13	72.11
	9/13/13	83.43
Bull	12/24/14	53.17 (a)
	1/23/15	58.52
	2/24/15	54.22
	4/30/15	71.78
	5/14/15	60.38
	12/27/15	99.21
	4/22/16	84.96
Bear	11/21/16	110.15
	2/2/17	87.01
	3/20/17	98.20
	11/8/17	68.58
	11/23/17	74.23
Bull	12/19/17	65.95
	2/19/18	82.08
	4/11/18	75.58
	5/15/18	84.04
	6/1/18	77.93
	10/18/18	89.07
	2/8/19	79.15
	7/14/19	112.23
	8/20/19	98.46
	11/3/19	119.62

(Note: (a) This is a new series, to be comparable, multiply preceding figures by 0.7339)

FIG.C4

DOW THEORY DATES (cont'd)

Bear	11/3/19	119.62
	12/22/19	103.55
	1/3/20	109.88
	2/25/20	89.98
	4/8/20	105.65
	5/19/20	87.36
	7/8/20	94.51
	8/10/20	83.20
	9/17/20	89.95
	12/21/20	66.75
	5/5/21	80.03
Bull	8/24/21	63.90
	12/15/21	81.50
	1/10/22	78.59
	5/29/22	96.41
	6/12/22	90.73
Bear	10/14/22	103.43
	11/27/22	92.03
	3/20/23	105.38
Bull	7/31/23	86.91
	8/29/23	93.70
	10/27/23	85.76
	2/6/24	101.31
	5/20/24	88.33
	8/20/24	105.57
	10/14/24	99.18
	3/6/25	125.68
	3/30/25	115.00
	2/11/26	162.31
	3/30/26	135.20
	8/14/26	166.64
	10/19/26	145.66
	10/3/27	199.78
	10/22/27	179.78
	5/14/28	220.88
	6/18/28	201.96
	11/28/28	295.62
	12/8/28	257.33
	2/5/29	322.06
	5/27/29	293.42
	9/3/29	381.17

Bear	9/3/29	381.17
	10/4/29	325.17
	10/10/29	352.86
	11/13/29	198.29
	4/17/30	294.07
	6/24/30	211.84
	9/10/30	245.09
	12/16/30	157.51
	2/24/31	194.36
	6/2/31	121.70
	6/27/31	156.93
	10/5/31	86.48
	11/9/31	116.79
	1/5/32	71.24
	3/8/32	88.78
Bull	7/8/32	41.22
	9/7/32	79.93
	2/27/33	50.16
	7/18/33	108.67
	10/21/33	83.64
	4/6/36	161.99
	4/29/36	143.65
Bear	3/10/37	194.40
	6/14/37	165.51
	8/14/37	190.02
	11/24/37	113.64
	1/11/38	134.35
Bull	3/31/38	98.95
	4/16/38	121.00
	5/31/38	107.74
	8/6/38	145.67
	9/26/38	129.91
Bear	11/12/38	158.41
	1/26/39	136.42
	3/10/39	152.28
Bull	4/8/39	121.44
	6/10/39	140.14
	6/29/39	130.05
	7/22/39	144.71
	8/24/39	131.33

FIG.C5

BASIC ELLIOTT

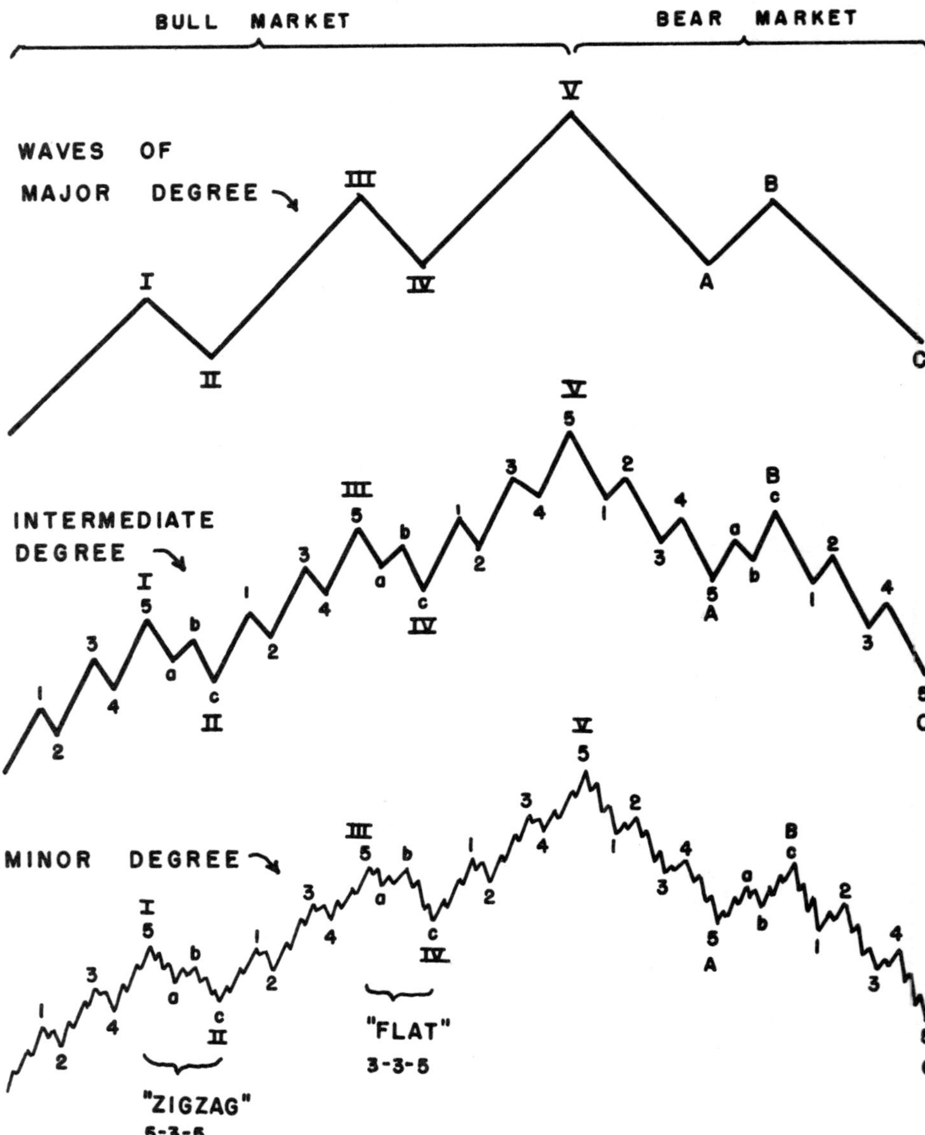

FIG.D1

Appendix D

WHAT IS THE ELLIOTT WAVE THEORY?

Some refreshing ideas about the behavior of Wall Street were developed by Ralph Nelson Elliott (1871-1948). We have reviewed all of his published writings, and have summarized them in this appendix.

Ralph Elliott spent many years in Latin America as an accountant. In 1927 he retired to Los Angeles where he developed his wave theories. These were published in 1938 in a monograph "The Wave Principle", in a series of articles in the Financial World in 1939, and in a book "Nature's Law" published in 1946. His ideas proved so interesting to investors that he came to New York and spent the last years of his life writing a financial report.

Basically, he believed that prices tend to fluctuate in natural ways. The most important tendencies, he believed, were founded on the Fibonacci series of numbers: 1-1-2-3-5-8-13-21-34-... Each number in this series is equal to the sum of the two preceding numbers, and the ratios are found many places in nature. The count of seeds in the whorls of sunflowers and pineapples are examples. Elliott found the numbers existing in the timing of waves and in the ratios of stock market prices at various turning points.

Elliott's most basic conclusions are illustrated by Fig.D1, which is derived from one he published in "Nature's Law." The tendency that he illustrates is simply that moves in the direction of trend tend to be in five swings; those in the contrary direction tend to be in three swings.

The top chart illustrates the "major" or primary waves in a bull and a bear market. The bull market has five swings; the bear market has three.

The center chart (Fig.D1) illustrates the tendency toward the breakdown of the primary waves into waves of the next smaller or "intermediate degree." Note that each major swing in the direction of trend (up in a bull market; down in a bear market) is made up of five swings of intermediate degree. These are marked 1,2,3,4,5. Each swing counter to trend is made of up three swings. These are marked a,b,c.

The lower chart is a continuation of the same basic tendency. The longer of the "Intermediate" swings is made up of five swings of minor degree; the shorter of the intermediate swings break down into three swings of minor degree. An exception is the swing marked "flat."

In Fig.D2 and Fig.D3 we have summarized and tabulated all of Elliott's various examples for the period 1929 through 1945. This period spans the time beginning with the first Dow Jones high-low statistics and ending with the last analysis published in "Nature's Law" a few months before his death. The nomenclature has been standardized, in order to make it easier for a student to trace through Elliott's interpretation of the wave patterns.

In addition to his basic conclusions, Elliott listed many variations, which are charted completely in Fig.D4 through D11.

He listed some subsidiary conclusions:

(1) No confirmation is required by a companion average. (The Dow Theory requires confirmation of the Industrials by the Rails.)

(2) Actual high and low figures are used, rather than the closing price. Elliott said "in fact it was only with the establishment of the daily range in 1928 and the hourly averages in 1932 that sufficient reliable data became available to establish the rhythmic recurrence of the phenomenon called "The Wave Principle."

(3) News has little effect on the course of a wave series. It may affect the amplitude and timing.

(4) Prices tend to move in channels. These can be useful in the interpretation of waves.

(5) Elliott listed his names for the degree of waves in the following order:

Subminuette (only in hourly data)
Minuette
Minute
Minor
Intermediate
Primary
Cycle
Super Cycle
Grand Super Cycle.

(6) There are many exceptions to the basic pattern.

Elliott's Waves

DATE	T.P. DEG.	WAVE
11/28/28	17.69	
3/26/29	15.27	A
5/6/29	14.13	1
5/31/29	14.13	2
9/3/29	851.92	B 3
11/13/29	52.16	1
4/16/30	52.16	2
5/5/30	10.97	a
5/14/30	10.97	b
6/25/30	19.00	c
9/10/30	19.00	d
12/17/30	27.52	3 e
2/24/31	27.52	4
10/5/31	39.34	a
11/9/31	39.34	b
1/5/32	28.62	c
2/19/32	28.62	d
7/8/32	851.92	I C 5 e
9/8/32	63.83	A
12/3/32	18.60	1
1/11/33	18.60	2
2/27/33	63.83	B 3
7/18/33	34.46	C
10/21/33	34.46	1
2/5/34	32.34	2
7/26/34	32.34	D 3
12/6/34	5.36	1
3/18/35	12.86	2
11/20/35	8.02	3
4/30/36	15.22	4
3/10/37	111.02	II E 5
6/17/37	16.58	A
8/14/37	16.58	B
8/27/37	2.29	1
8/31/37	2.29	2
9/13/37	6.73	3
9/30/37	7.45	4
10/19/37	21.91	C 5
10/21/37	10.65	a
10/25/37	10.65	b
10/29/37	21.91	1 c
11/23/37	19.91	2
1/15/38	19.91	3
2/4/38	13.43	4
2/23/38	13.43	D 5
3/12/38	4.66	1
3/15/38	4.66	2
3/23/38	2.83	3
3/24/38	2.83	4
3/31/38	63.04	III E 5

DATE	T.P. DEG.	WAVE
4/18/38	14.19	1
5/27/38	14.19	2
7/25/38	14.44	3
9/28/38	14.44	4
11/10/38	63.04	A 5
1/26/39	12.20	1
3/10/39	12.20	2
4/11/39	31.43	B 3
6/9/39	9.13	1
6/30/39	9.13	2
8/3/39	14.30	3
9/1/39	14.30	4
9/13/39	31.43	IV C 5
1/15/40	6.31	1
4/8/40	6.31	2
6/10/40	25.69	A 3
8/12/40	5.50	1
8/16/40	5.50	2
11/8/40	25.69	B 3
5/1/41	14.22	1
7/22/41	14.22	2
12/24/41	8.95	3
1/6/42	8.95	4
4/28/42	111.02	V C 5
7/15/42	4.78	I
8/5/42	4.78	II
11/9/42	4.16	A
11/24/42	4.16	B
4/6/43	5.90	C
4/13/43	5.90	D
7/15/43	13.55	III E
8/2/43	6.45	A
9/20/43	6.45	B
11/30/43	13.55	IV C
1/11/44	3.57	1
4/25/44	4.96	2
7/10/44	5.86	A 3
9/7/44	5.86	B
10/6/44	2.78	1
11/16/44	2.78	2
3/6/45	6.91	3
3/26/45	6.91	4
6/26/45	6.00	C 5
7/27/45	6.00	D
12/10/45	4.84	V E

FIG. D2

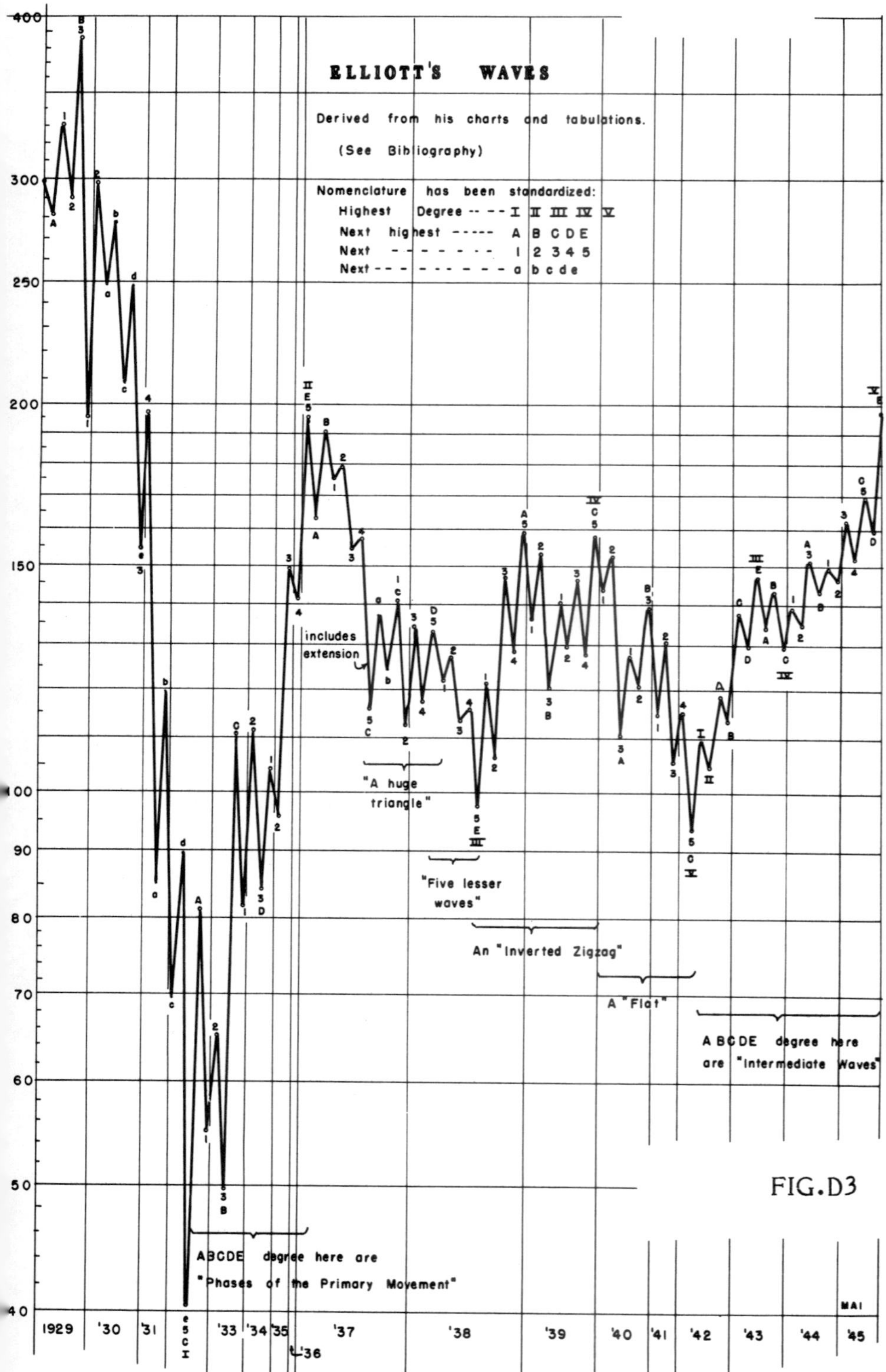
ELLIOTT'S WAVES
Derived from his charts and tabulations.
(See Bibliography)
Nomenclature has been standardized:
Highest Degree ---- I II III IV V
Next highest ----- A B C D E
Next -------- 1 2 3 4 5
Next ---------- a b c d e
"A huge triangle"
"Five lesser waves"
An "Inverted Zigzag"
A "Flat"
ABCDE degree here are "Intermediate Waves"
ABCDE degree here are "Phases of the Primary Movement"
includes extension

FIG.D3

ELLIOTT VARIATIONS - IN LINE OF TREND-

Elliott found that waves in the line of trend (1, 3, 5) sómetimes elongated into five waves of the same degree - rather than breaking down into five waves of a lower degree. This elongation could occur in waves 1, 3, or 5, but not in waves 2 or 4. It usually occurred in the last or fifth wave. He called these elongations extensions.

Extension in Wave 1, upward trend.

Extension in Wave 1, downward trend.

Extension in Wave 3, upward trend.

Extension in Wave 3 downward trend

Extension in Wave 5, upward trend.

Extension in Wave 5, downward trend.

FIG.D4

ELLIOTT VARIATIONS - IN LINE OF TREND

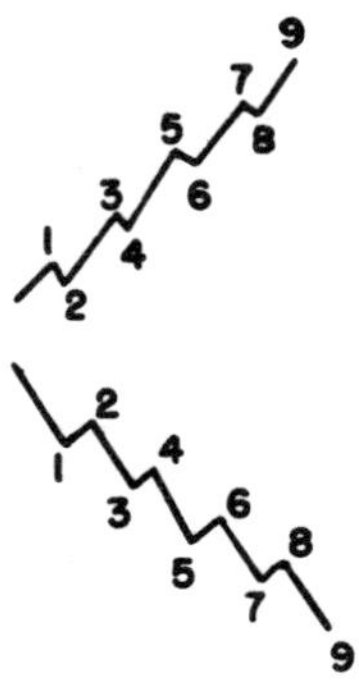

Figure 52.

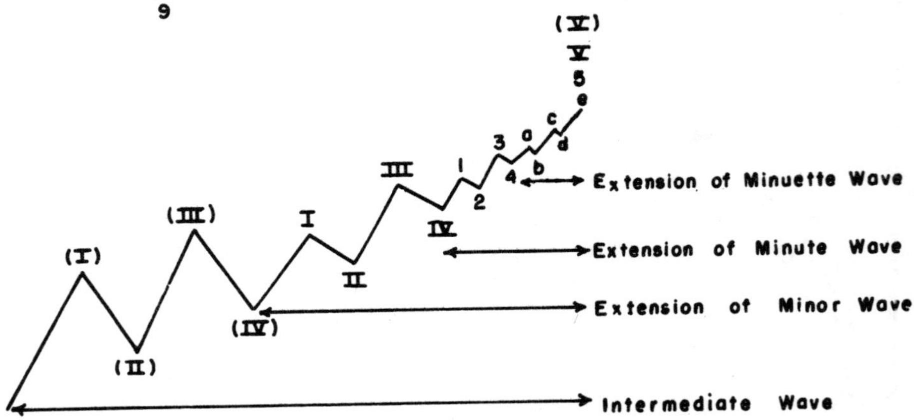

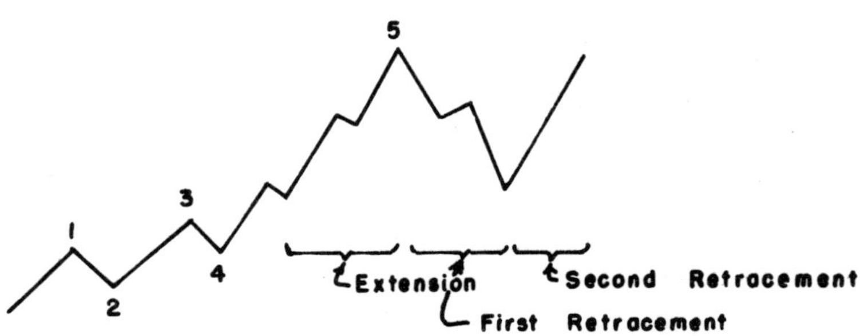

FIG.D5

Since extensions are comparable with the other waves in a series, they may be equal to them and the entire movement may seem to be nine waves of about equal size. (top chart, Fig.D5)

At the end of a major move, there may be a series of extensions of extensions in the fifth wave. The move comes to an end finally on the last minuette wave of the last minute wave of the last minor wave of the last intermediate wave. (middle chart)

Elliott found that extensions tend to be "double-retraced" i.e. by a downward and then by an upward move. (lower chart) This is interesting only in an extension of the fifth wave, since an extension in the first wave is retraced by the second and third waves and an extension in the third wave is retraced by the fourth and fifth waves.

ELLIOTT VARIATIONS - CORRECTIONS

ZIGZAGS

Elliott recognized corrections of five types: zigzag, flat, irregular, triangular, and complex. They will be illustrated by Figures 55. through 60.

Three sizes of "Zigzags" are illustrated by Figure 55. In the minor size, each wave is single; in the intermediate size the distribution is the usual 5-3-5 found in the "Basic Elliott" chart Figure 24. In the major size the two longer waves are doubled.

Note that the "inverted" versions are included. These are corrections of a downward trend.

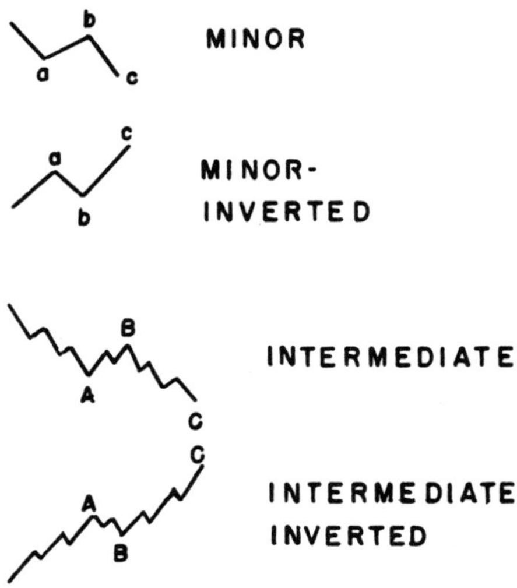

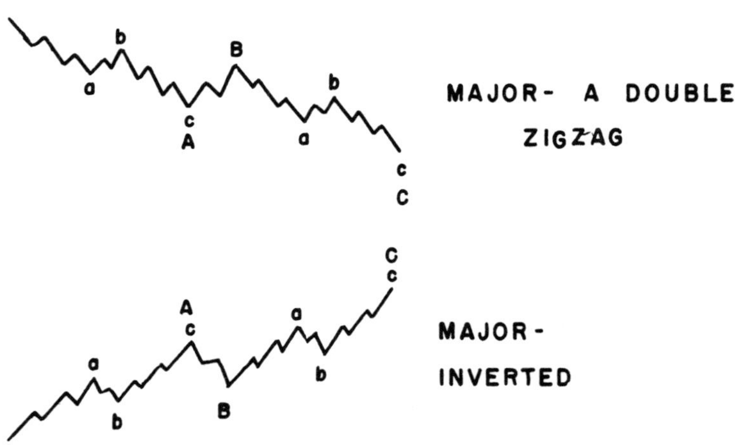

FIG.D6

ELLIOTT VARIATIONS - CORRECTIONS

FLATS

In a zigzag the pattern is 5-3-5; in a flat it is 3-3-5. This gives the "flat" correction a level appearance - and its name.

Examples of this correction are in this Figure 56. An example is marked in Figure 24., with a "zigzag" also marked for comparison.

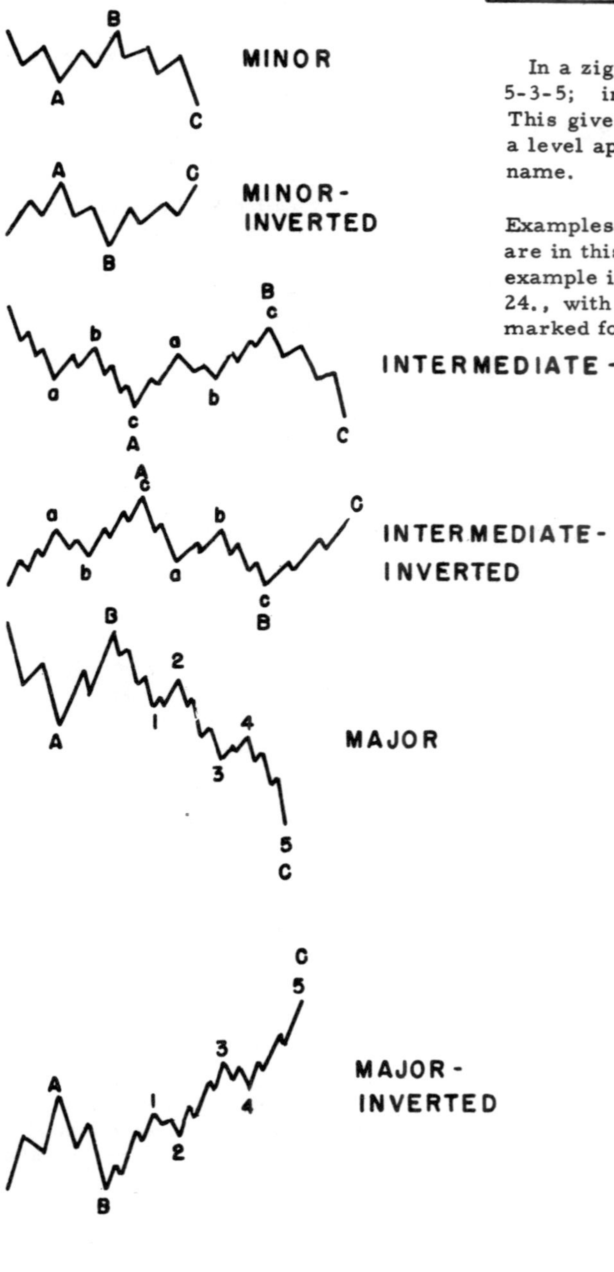

FIG.D7

ELLIOTT VARIATIONS - CORRECTIONS

IRREGULAR

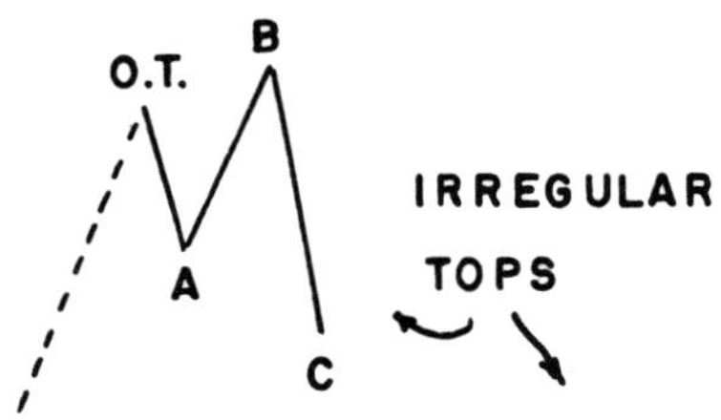

"Irregular corrections" are distinguished by the height of the "B" wave, which advances to another top higher than the orthodox top ("O. T.").

Since the correction makes a new top, it is also called an "irregular top". An example is the 1929 peak.

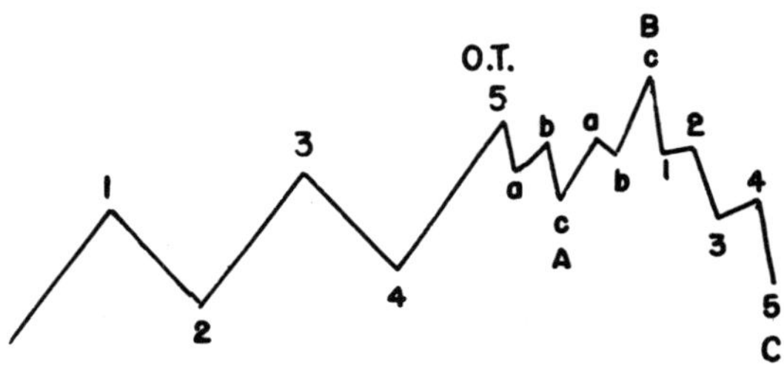

Normally "C" terminates below the bottom of "A". Liquidation in the third or "C" wave is usually more intensive than in the first wave.

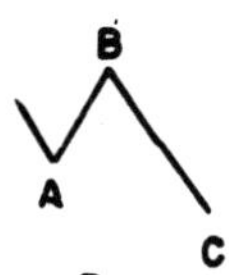

MINOR

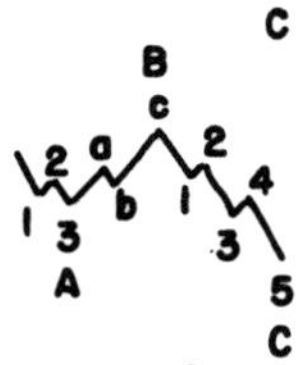

INTERMEDIATE

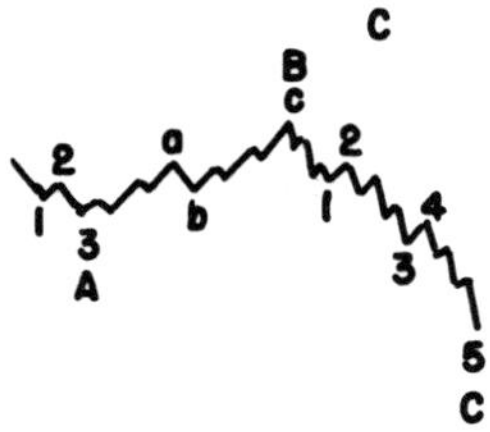

MAJOR

(In the larger and more important corrections the "C" wave may consist of three smaller five-wave sets.)

FIG. D8

ELLIOTT VARIATIONS - CORRECTIONS

TRIANGLES

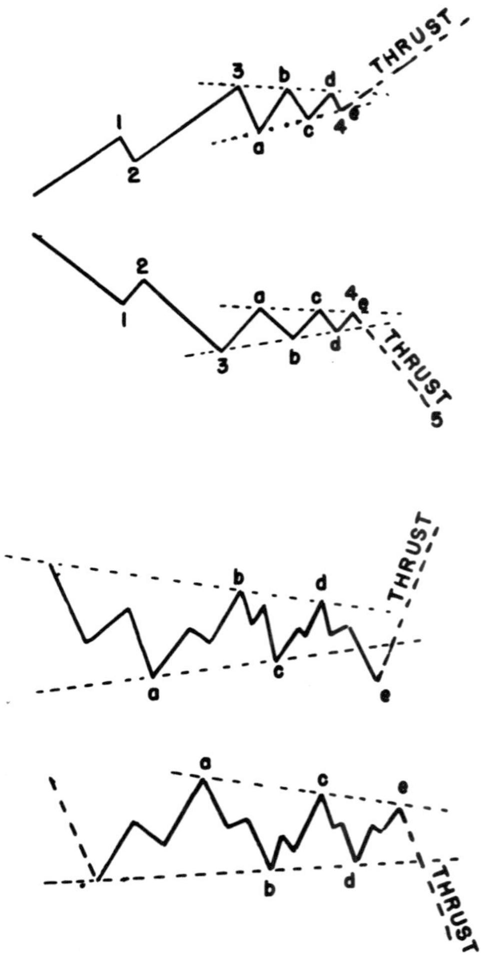

FIG.D9

Triangular corrections have five waves or legs each of which has no more than three lesser waves. In the small triangles the legs can be single waves.

Triangles are found in the fourth wave of a five wave movement - exclusively. They form the base for the fifth wave or "thrust".

One of the boundaries of a triangle may be horizontal. The fifth leg may terminate within or outside of the boundaries.

Triangles have been as short as seven hours (a short example is in Figure 59.) and as long as 13 years. A. Hamilton Bolton has outlined a 21. year triangle in his analyses.

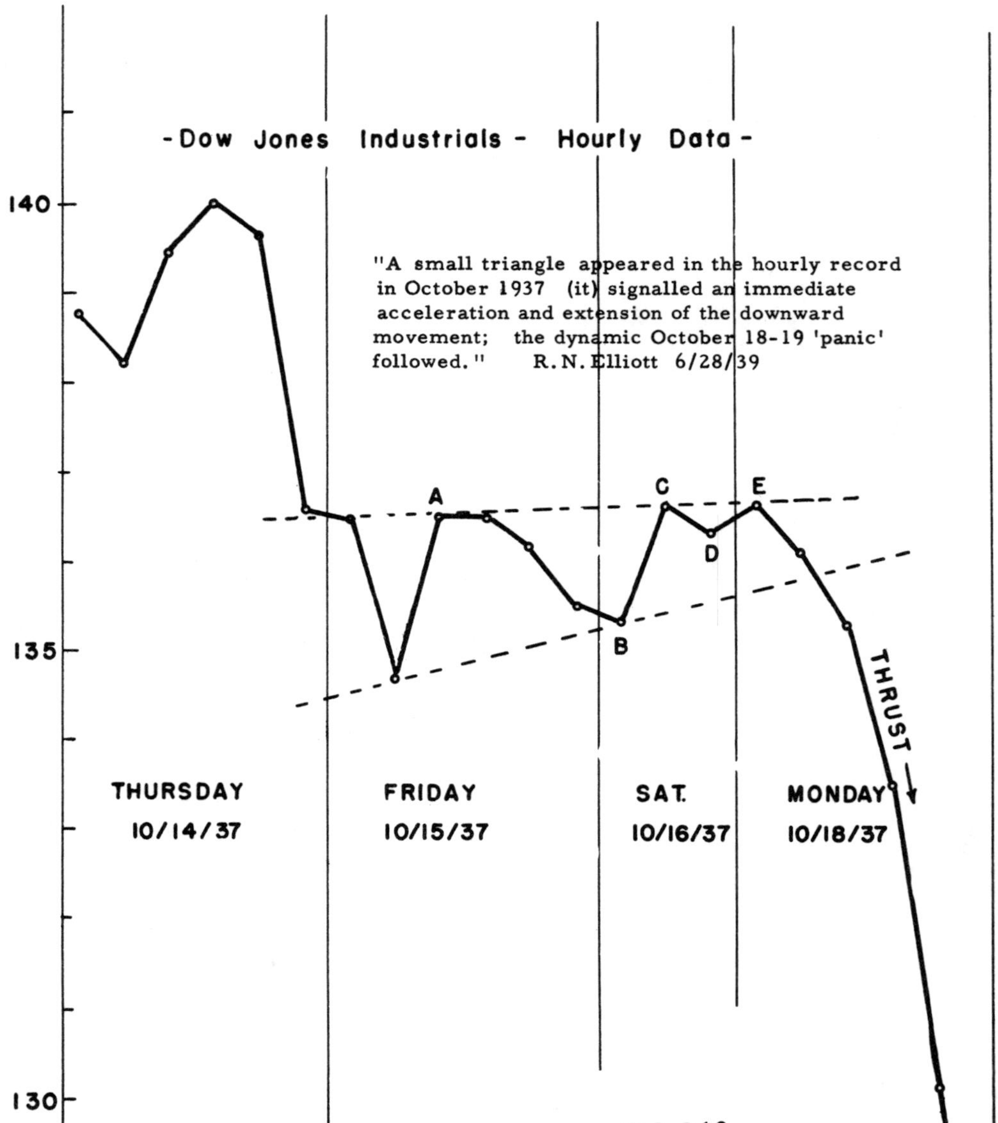
-Dow Jones Industrials - Hourly Data -
140
135
130
"A small triangle appeared in the hourly record in October 1937 (it) signalled an immediate acceleration and extension of the downward movement; the dynamic October 18-19 'panic' followed." R.N. Elliott 6/28/39
A
B
C
D
E
THRUST
THURSDAY
10/14/37
FRIDAY
10/15/37
SAT.
10/16/37
MONDAY
10/18/37

FIG.D10

ELLIOTT VARIATIONS — CORRECTIONS

COMPLEX

DOUBLE THREE

This group includes some final complex variations. In the words of Elliott: "The rhythm of corrective movements is the most difficult feature of the wave principle."

TRIPLE THREE

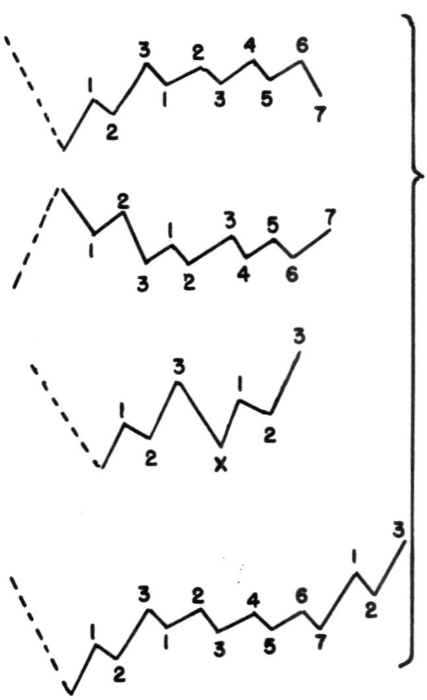

DOUBLE THREES

MIXED-UPWARD &

DOWNWARD

FIG.D11

Elliott had some problems in the application of his principle. Many of his turning points were debatable; his wave patterns tend to proliferate into variations.

The selection of turning points is crucial. You can identify almost any pattern if you select the proper turning points. If a filter is applied, some of Elliott's waves appear to be quite light, and he seems to have missed some important turns.

Another problem is the division of waves into subwaves. You can divide a wave into almost any number of subwaves, if you make the subwaves small enough.

We have tried to read Elliott's mind, from his limited writings, in order to develop a basis for measured analysis.

(1) In the breakdown of waves into subwaves, the first and most promising line of attack is a study of Elliott's own examples. The turning points that he used have been tabulated, using the method outlined in Appendix B.

(2) A second line of attack is a study of the "basic Ellliott" chart in Fig.D1. This chart outlines a complete cycle. If you will count the number of waves of major degree, intermediate degree, and minor degree, you will find the following:

Major degree:	8 waves
Intermediate degree	34 waves(4.25 as many)
Minor degree	142 waves (4.18 times as many as in the intermediate degree)

Using this as a guide, we counted down the rank of turning point evaluations:

filter:	number of turning points:
80%	4.0
40%	10.
20%	44.
10%	170.
5%	540.

The frequencies in the Basic Elliott chart of 8,34 and 142 are similar in proportion to the actual count in the selected groups of 10,44, and 170.

(3) A third possible approach is based on Elliott's statement that "a wave is divided into waves of the next smaller degree." If waves (or turning points) are ranked in any given period of time, from the highest filter to the lowest, and the rank is scanned downward, you will find at a certain point that the waves are parts of preceding waves. This is evidence that you are moving into a subwave classification.

For example, the ten most important turning points in the period 1928-1962 are the following:

Rank:	Date:	Filter:
(1)	09 03 29	829.00
(2)	07 08 32	829.00
(3)	03 06 37	109.29
(4)	04 28 42	109.29
(5)	09 08 32	60.85
(6)	02 27 33	60.85
(7)	03 31 38	60.42
(8)	11 10 38	60.42
(9)	11 13 29	48.00
(10)	04 16 30	48.00

You will find that numbers (7) and (8) are, in time, between (3) and (4), and evidently form a subwave. Numbers (9) and (10) are between (1) and (2) and evidently form a subwave. A similar method was used to check the other groupings.

The three approaches outlined above were combined and cross checked to yield the following filters to help in classification:

	Filter:	Elliott Wave:
Cycle	80	I,II,III,IV...
Primary	40	A,B,C,D...
Intermediate	20	1,2,3,4...
Minor	10	a,b,c,d...
Minute	5	

For more details, see "Elliott Wave Principle" by Prechter and Frost (App.J)

Appendix E -- Dow Jones Industrials Weekly --

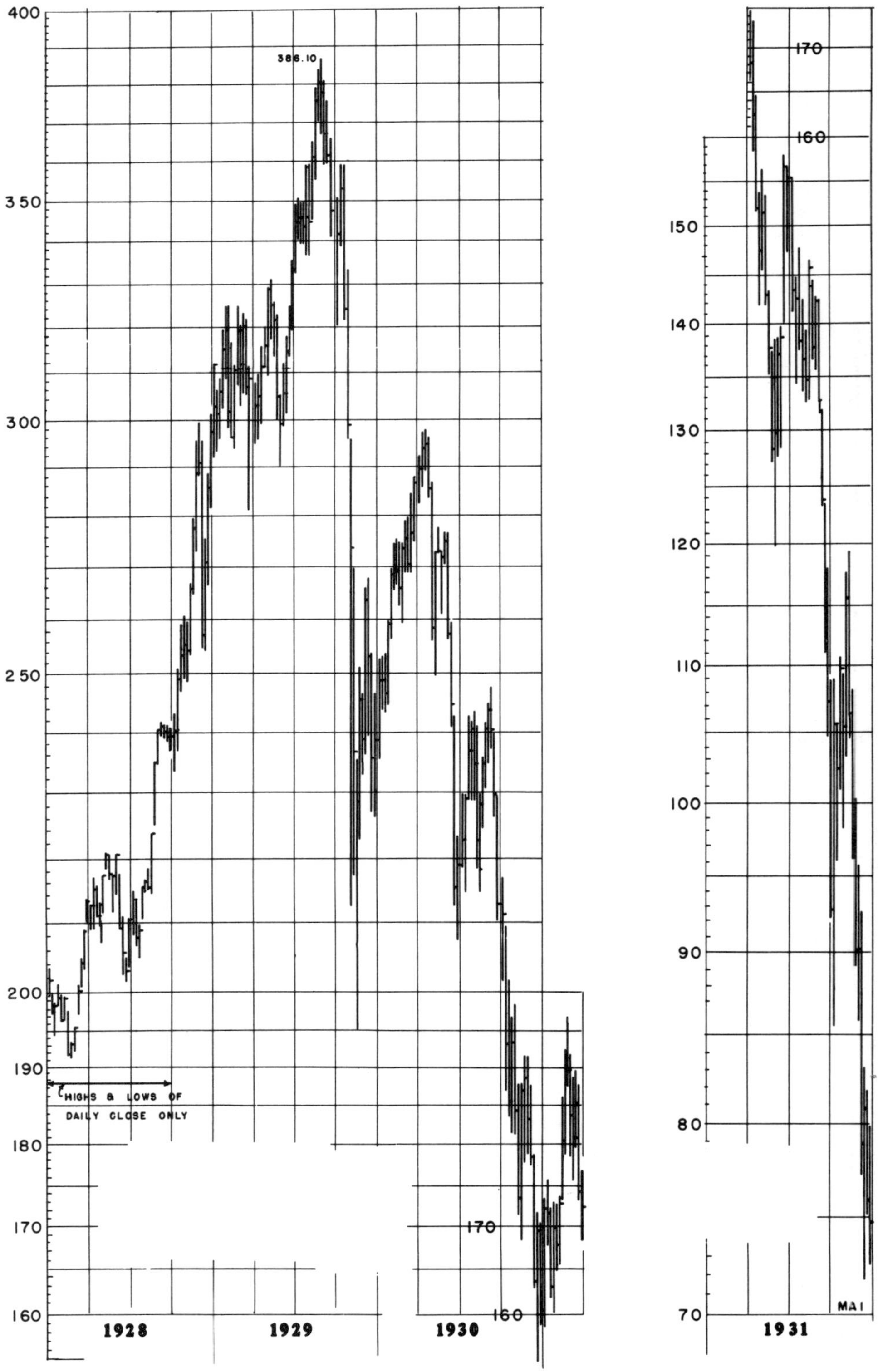

Appendix E -- Dow Jones Industrials Weekly --

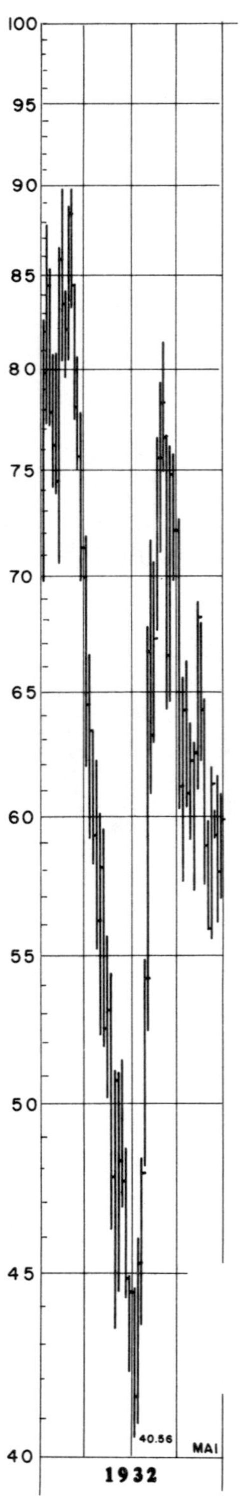

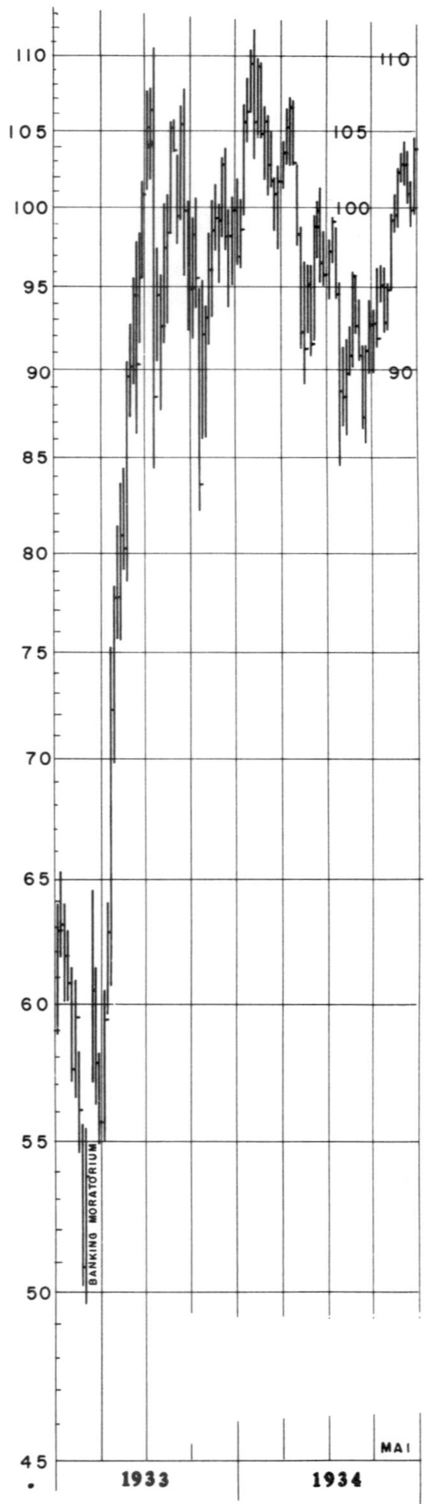

Appendix E -- Dow Jones Industrials Weekly --

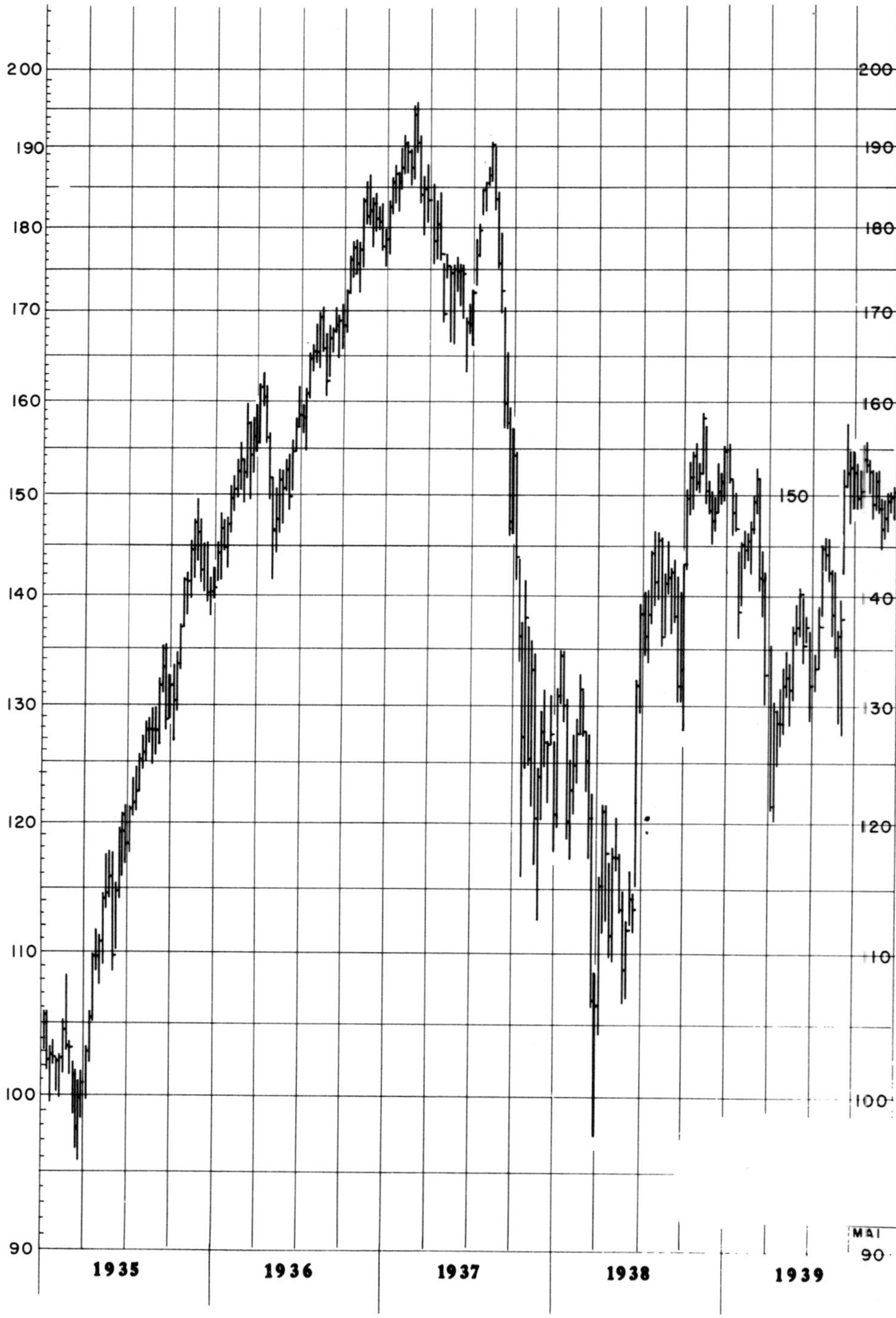

Appendix E -- Dow Jones Industrials Weekly --

Appendix E -- Dow Jones Industrials Weekly --

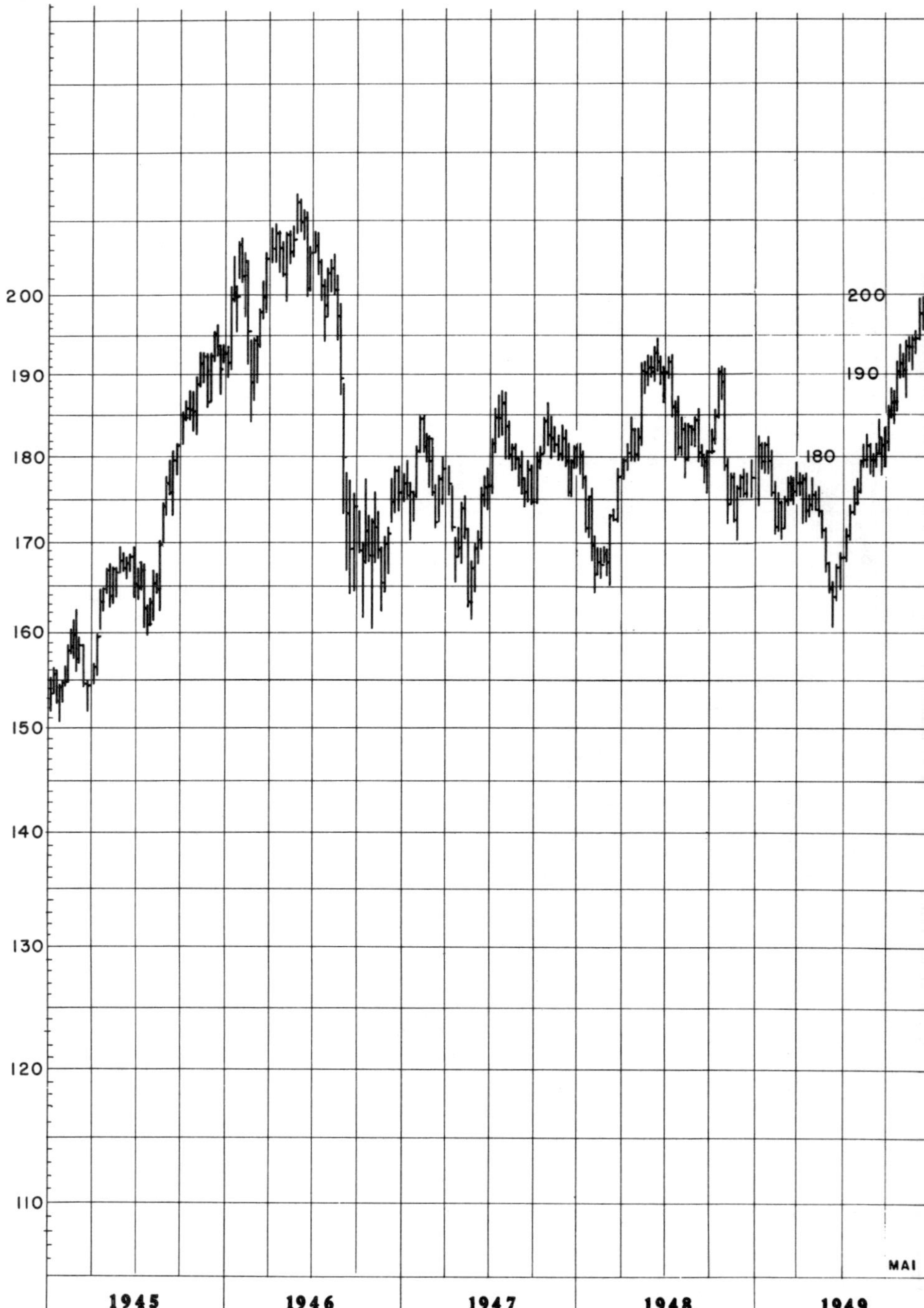

Appendix E -- Dow Jones Industrials Weekly --

Appendix E -- Dow Jones Industrials Weekly --

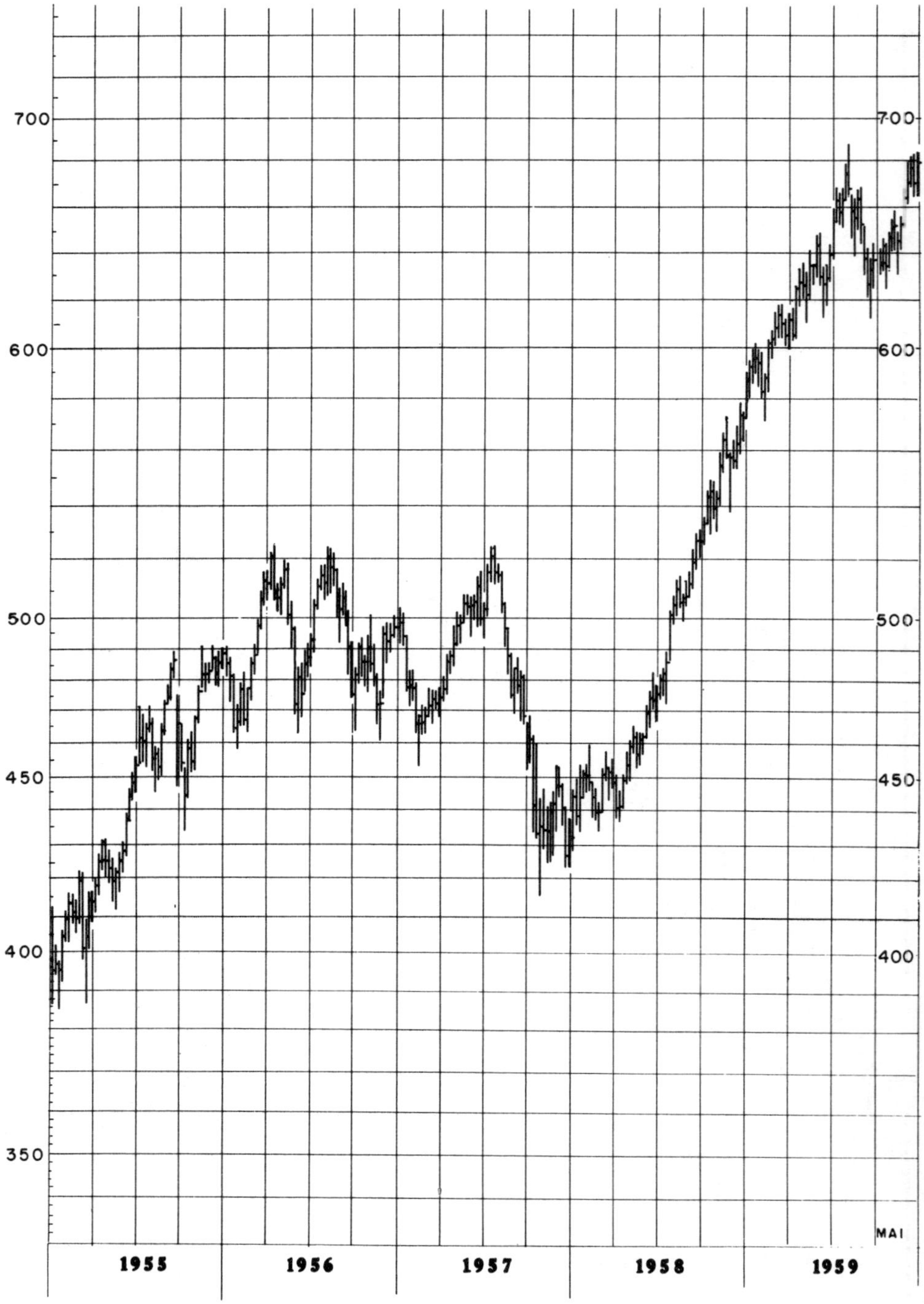

Appendix E -- Dow Jones Industrials Weekly --

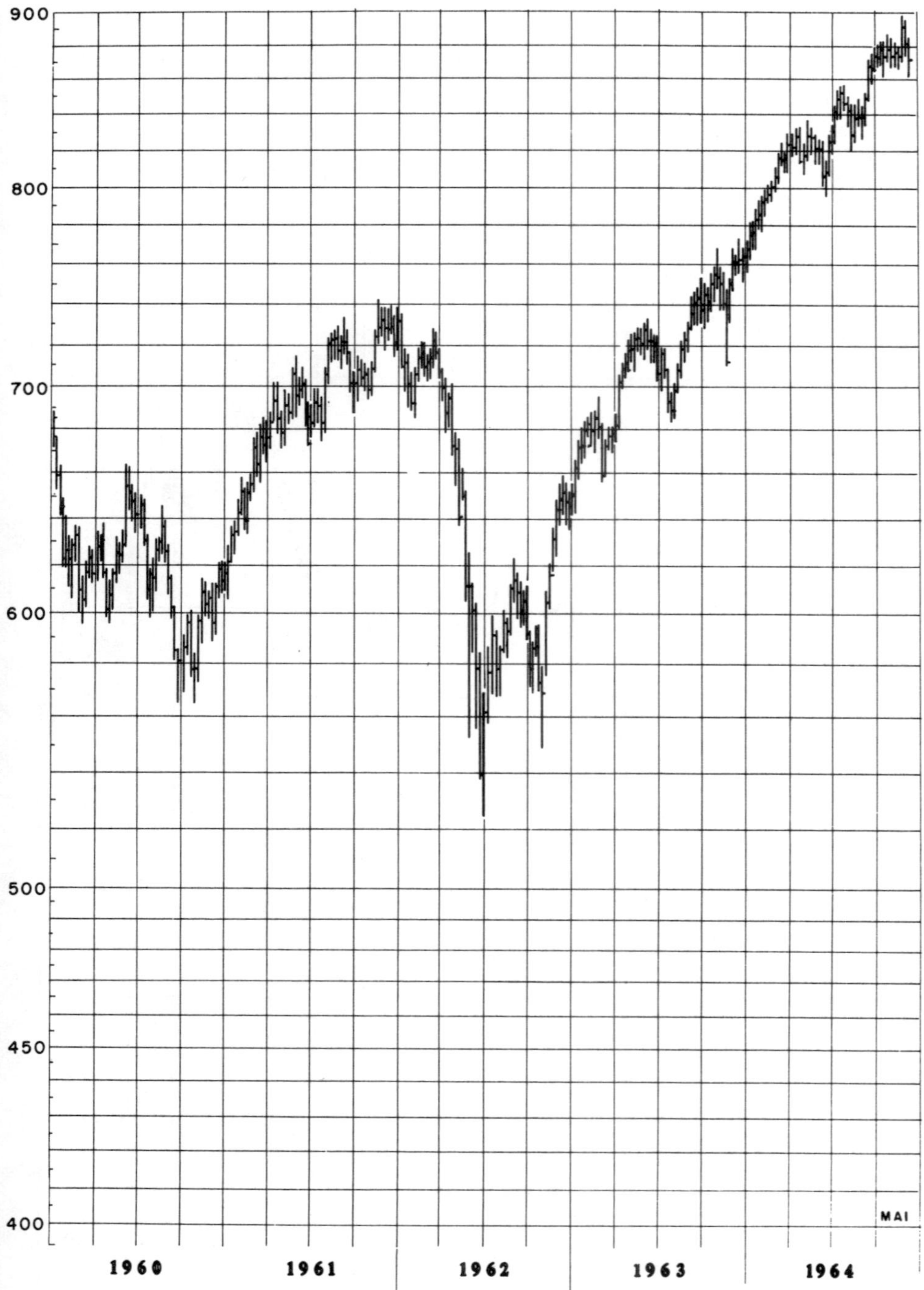

Appendix E -- Dow Jones Industrials Weekly --

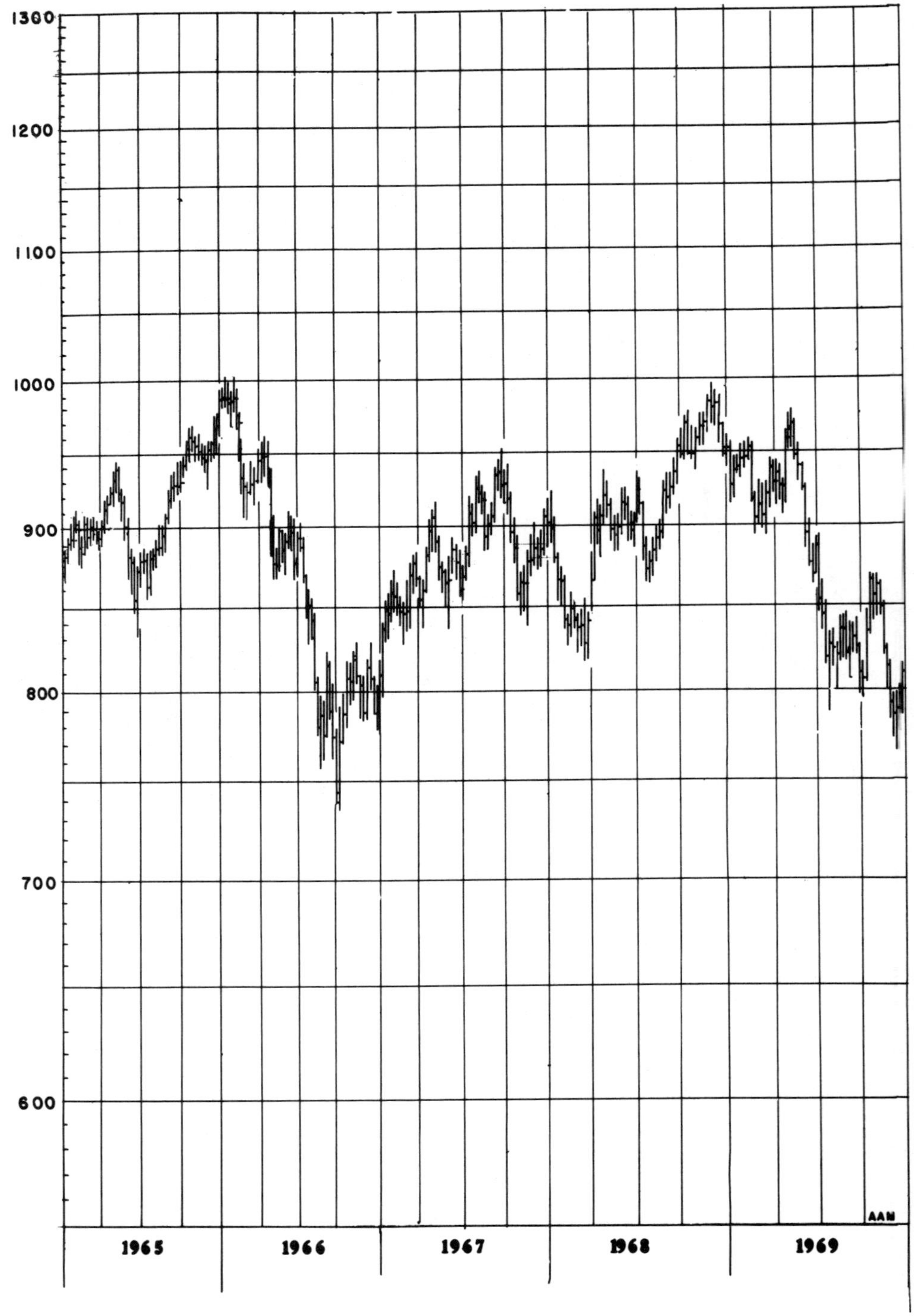

Appendix E -- Dow Jones Industrials Weekly --

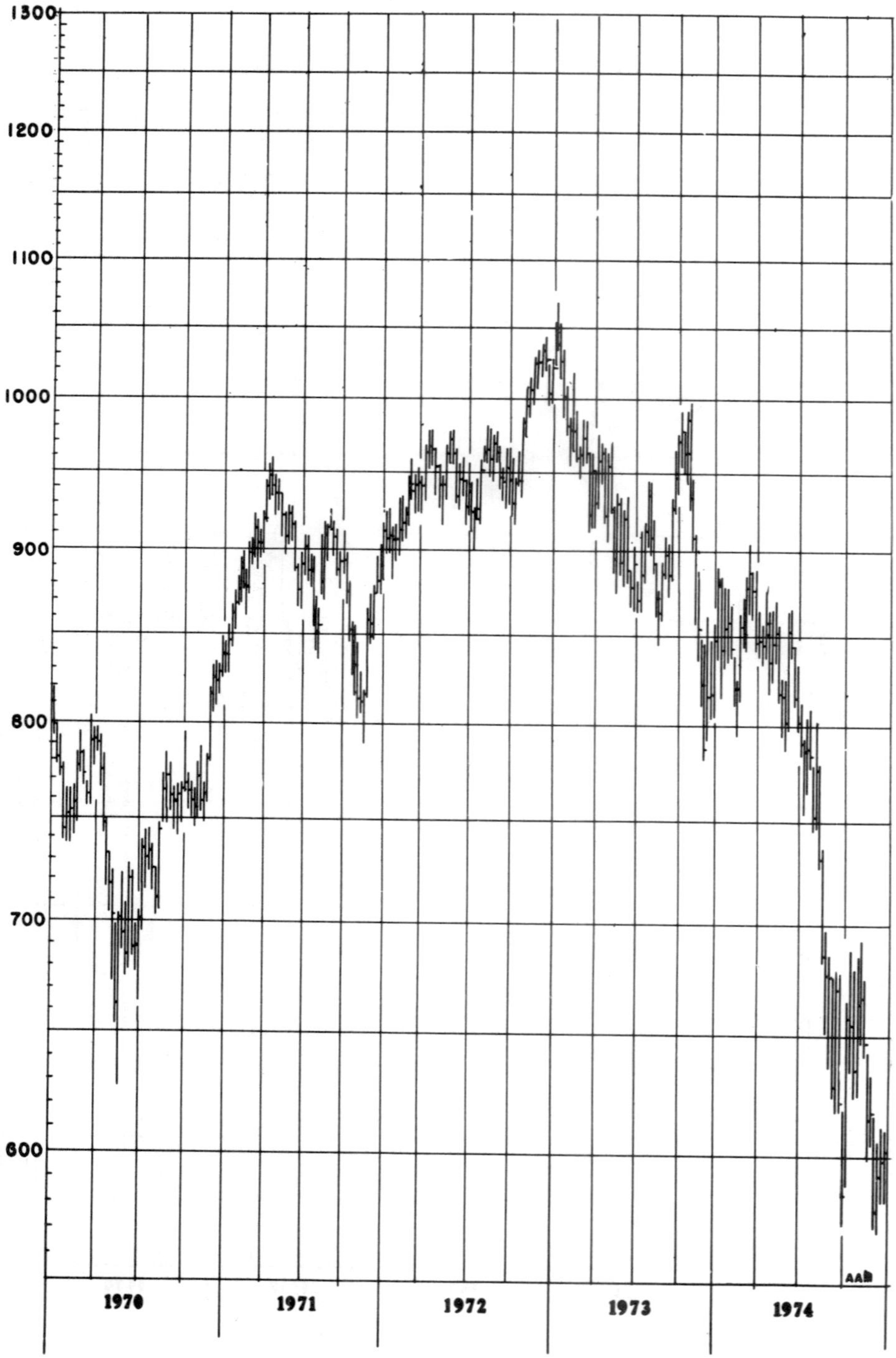

Appendix E -- Dow Jones Industrials Weekly --

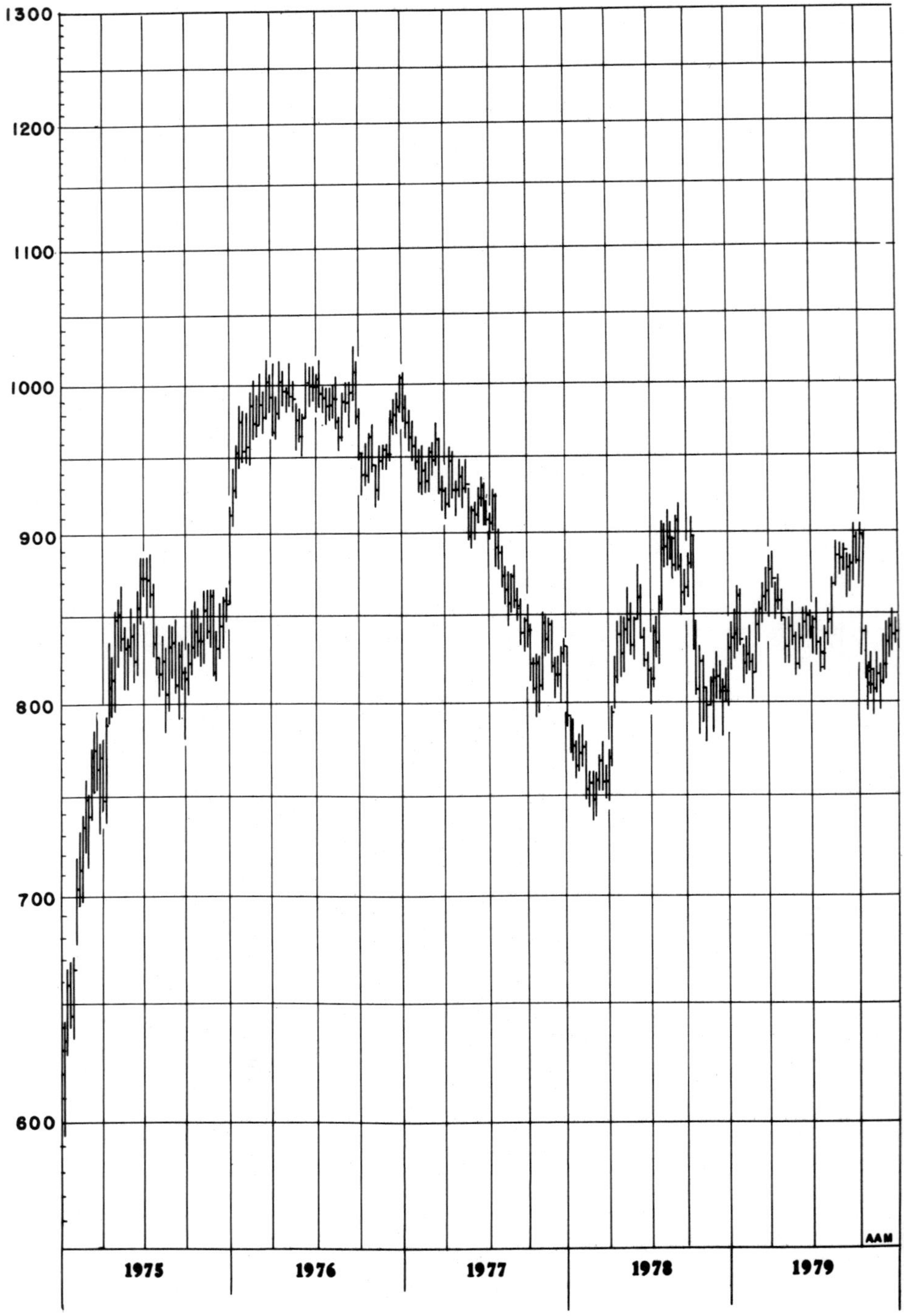

Appendix E -- Dow Jones Industrials Weekly --

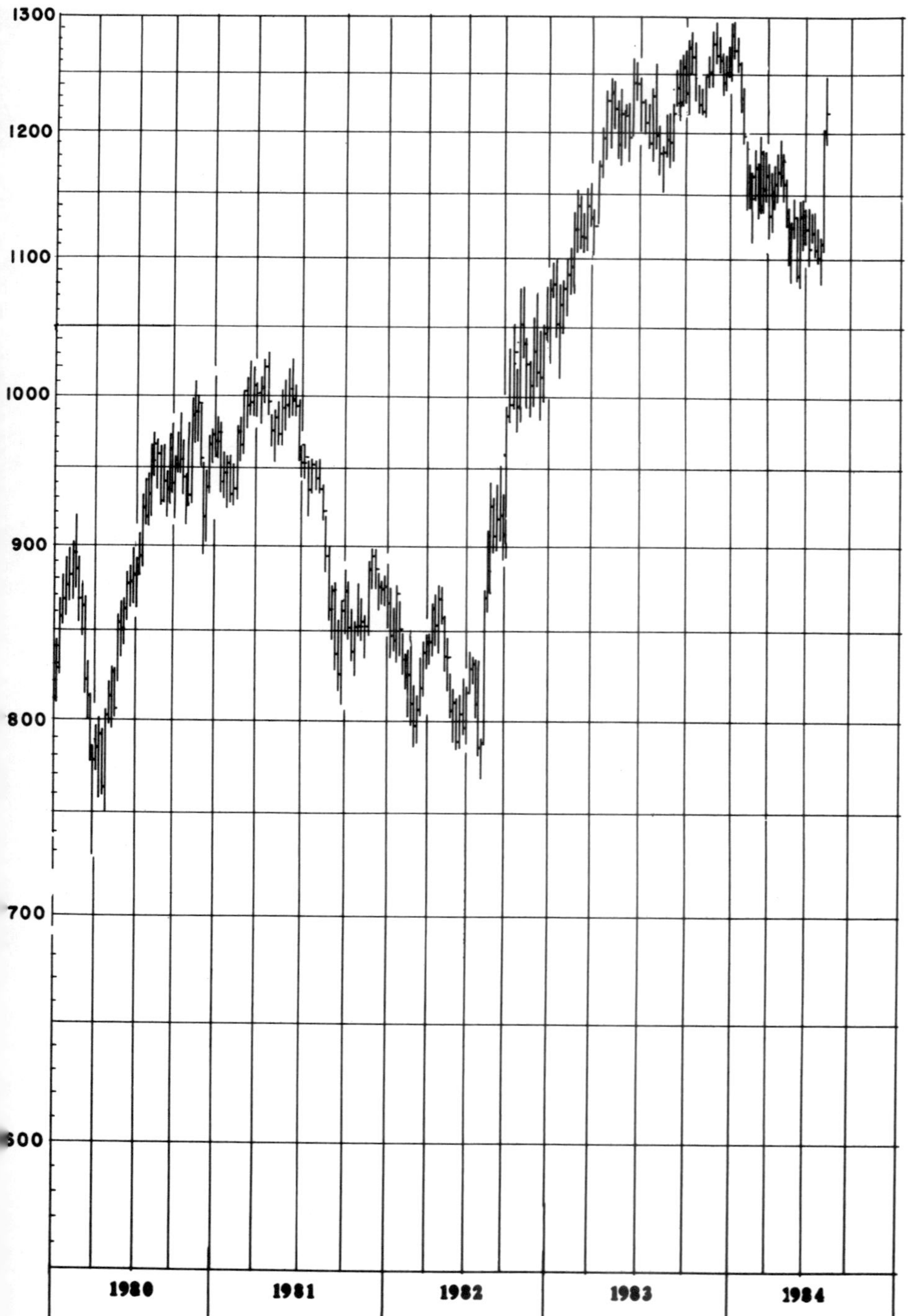

Appendix F
--Dow Jones Industrials, all swings over 5% --

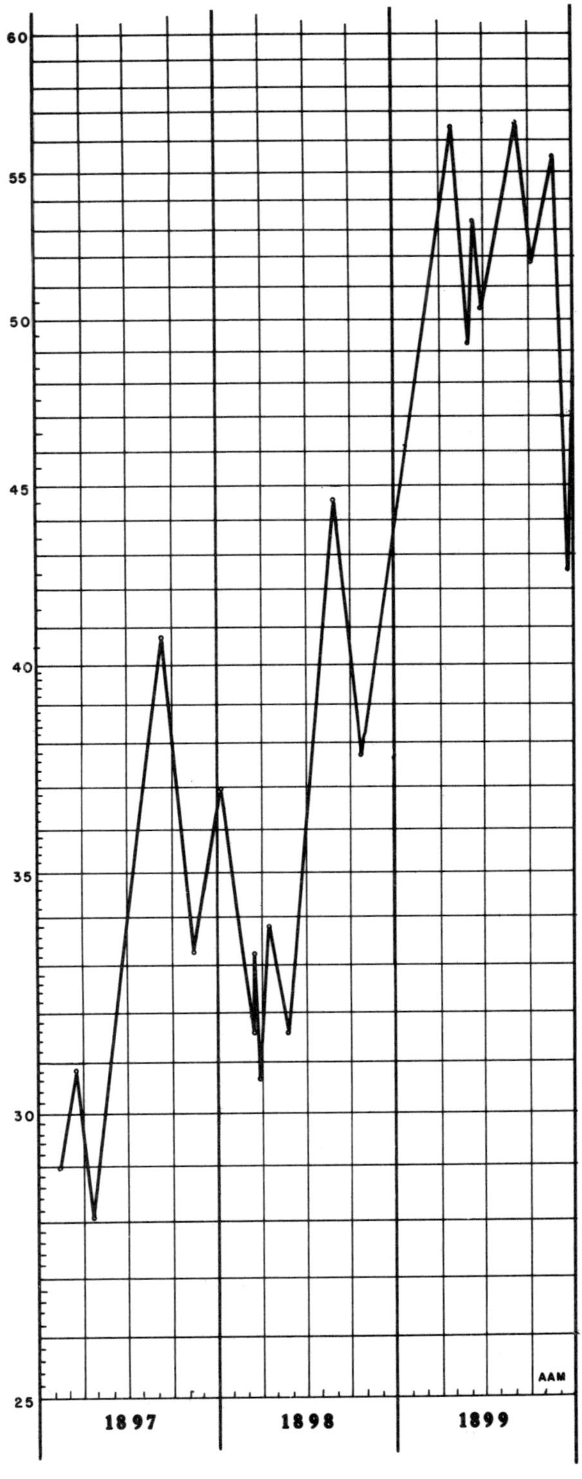

Appendix F
--Dow Jones Industrials, all swings over 5% --

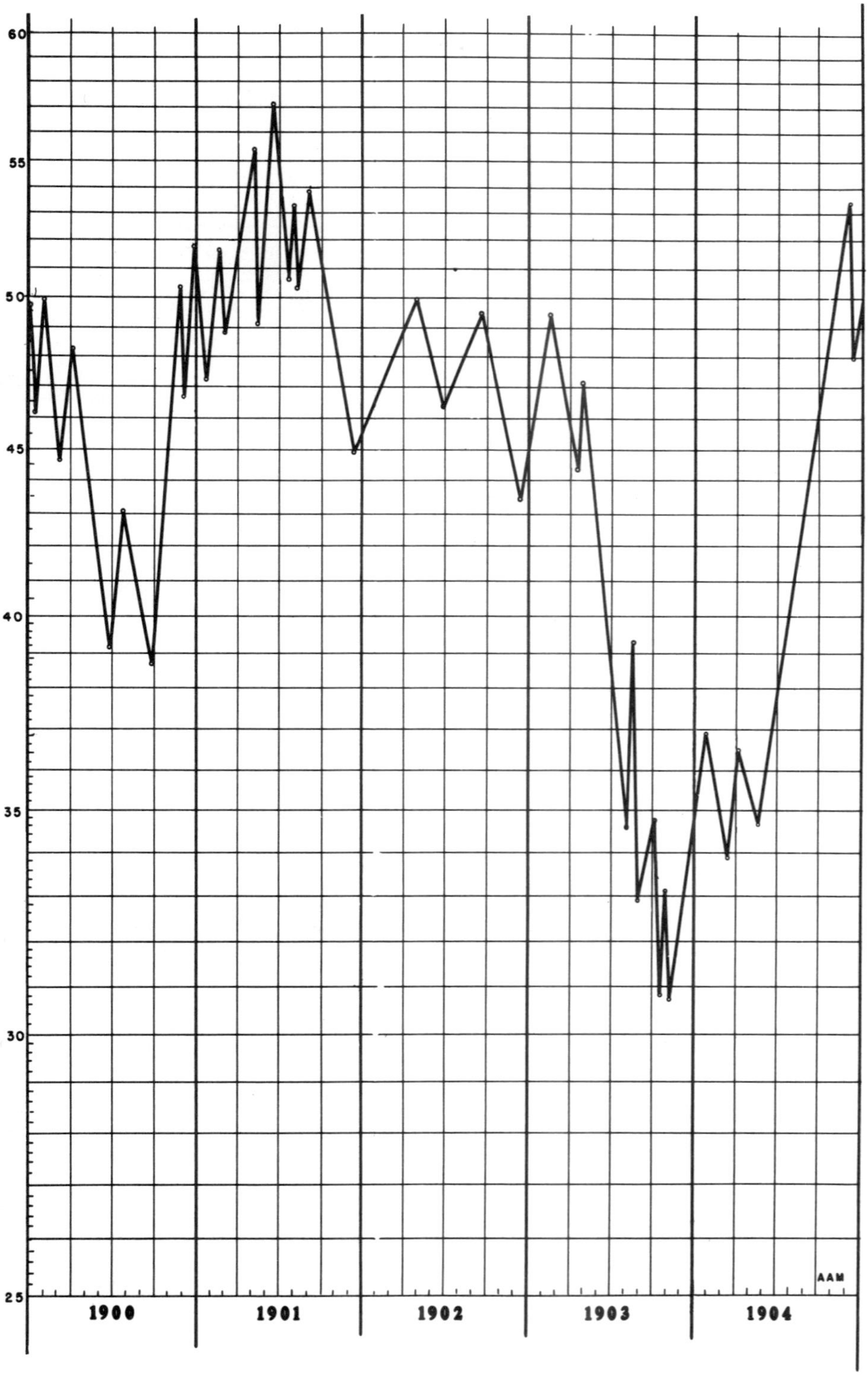

Appendix F
--Dow Jones Industrials, all swings over 5% --

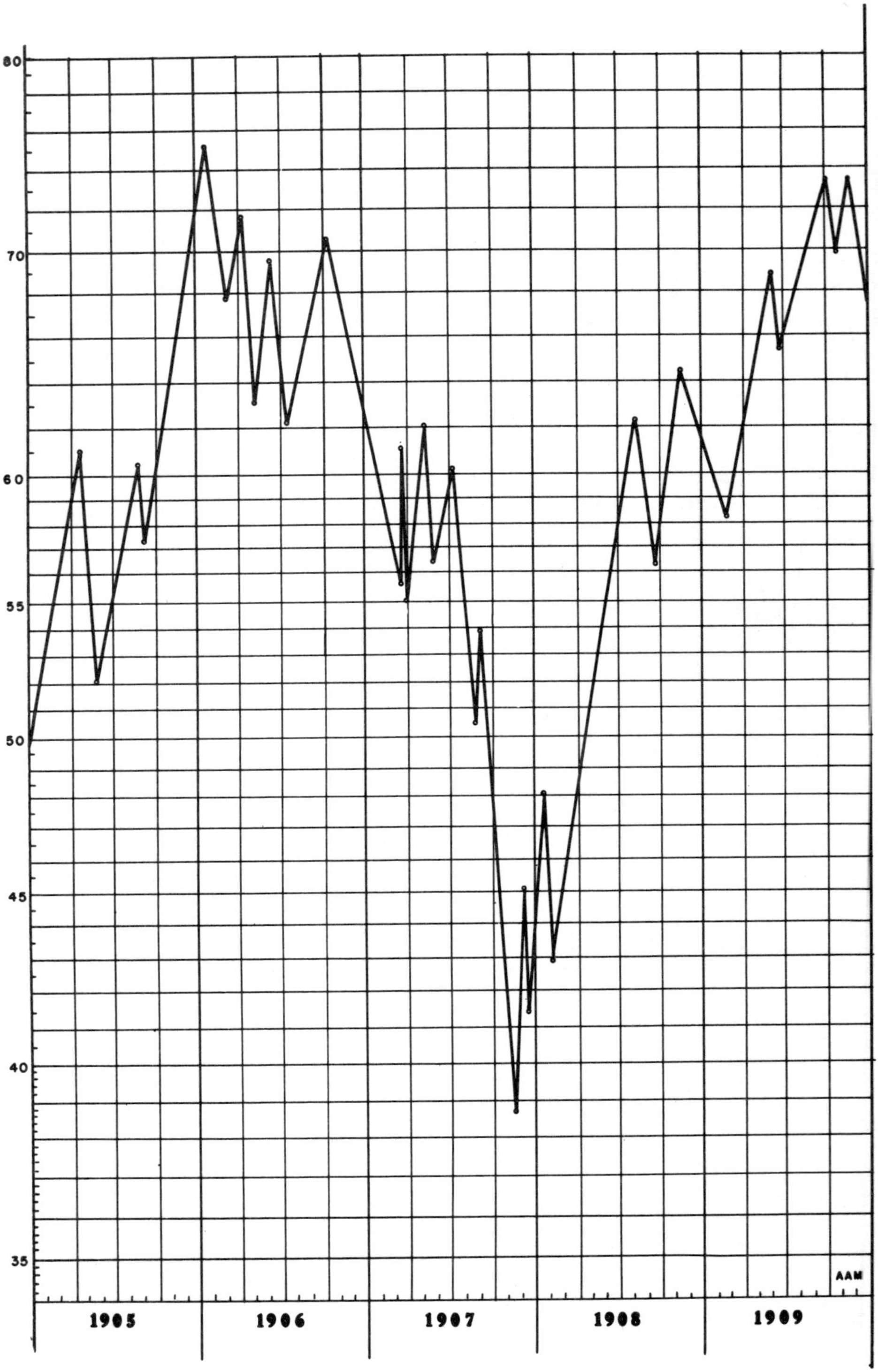

Appendix F
--Dow Jones Industrials, all swings over 5% --

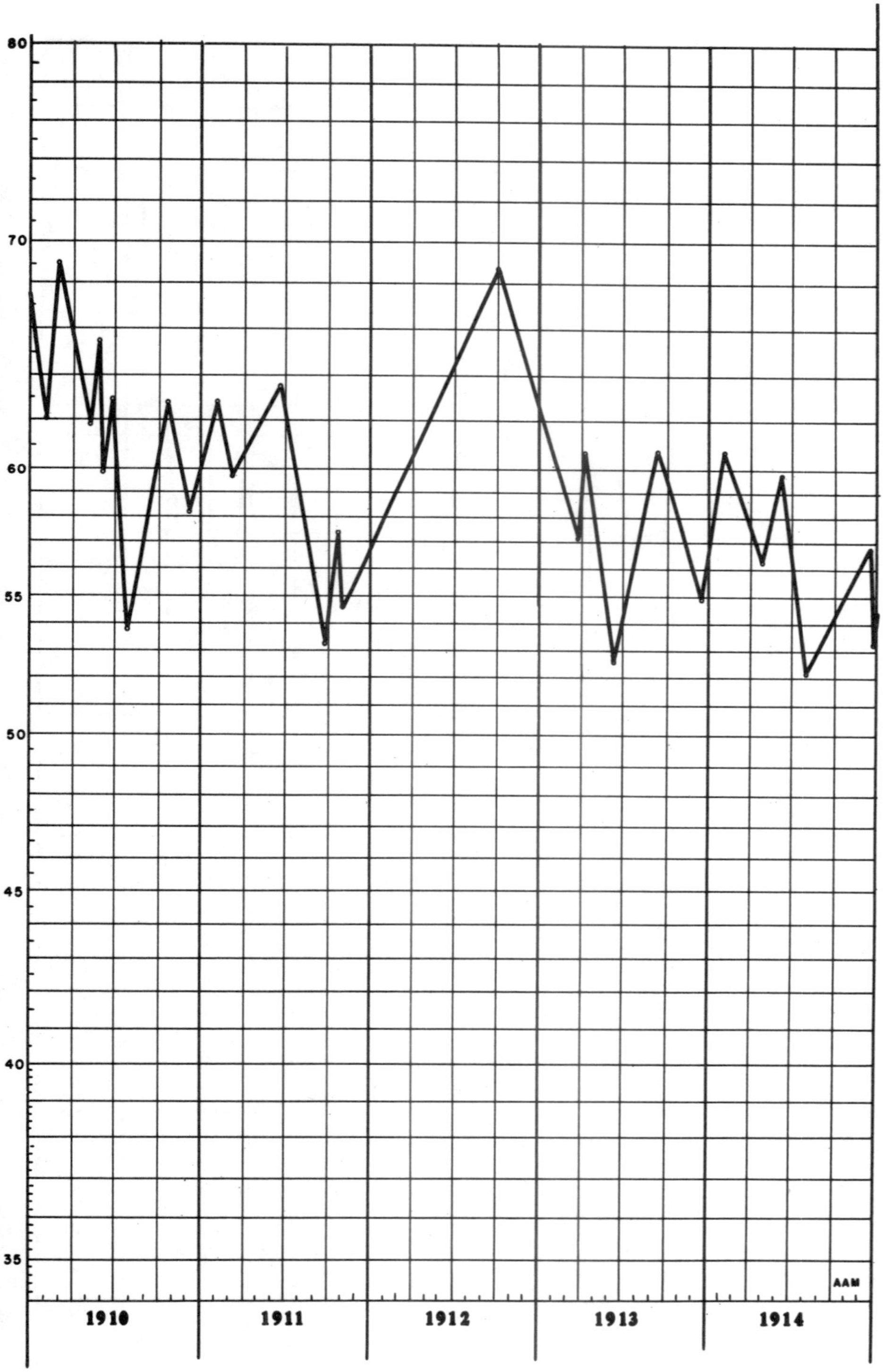

Appendix F
--Dow Jones Industrials, all swings over 5% --

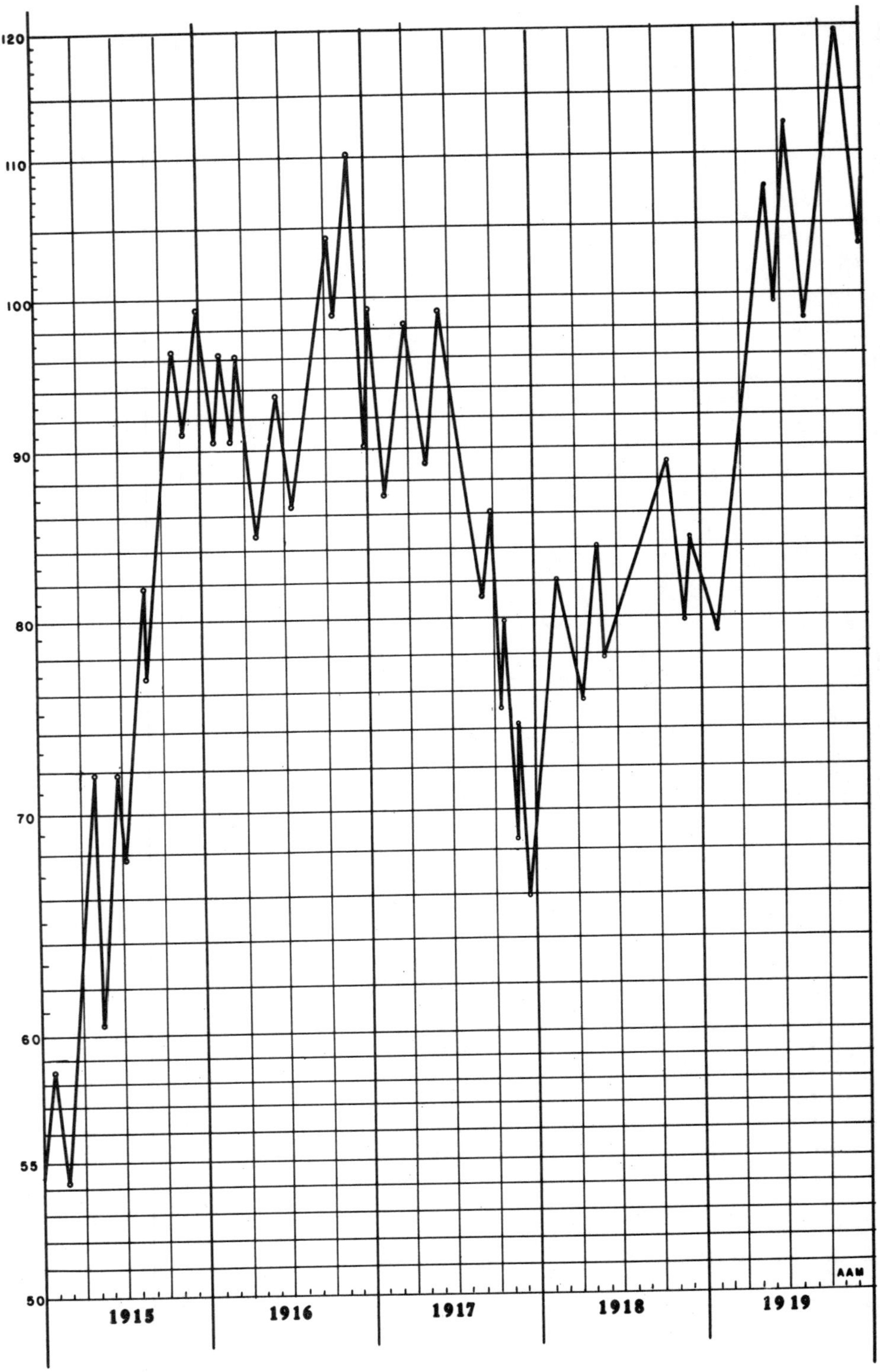

Appendix F
--Dow Jones Industrials, all swings over 5% --

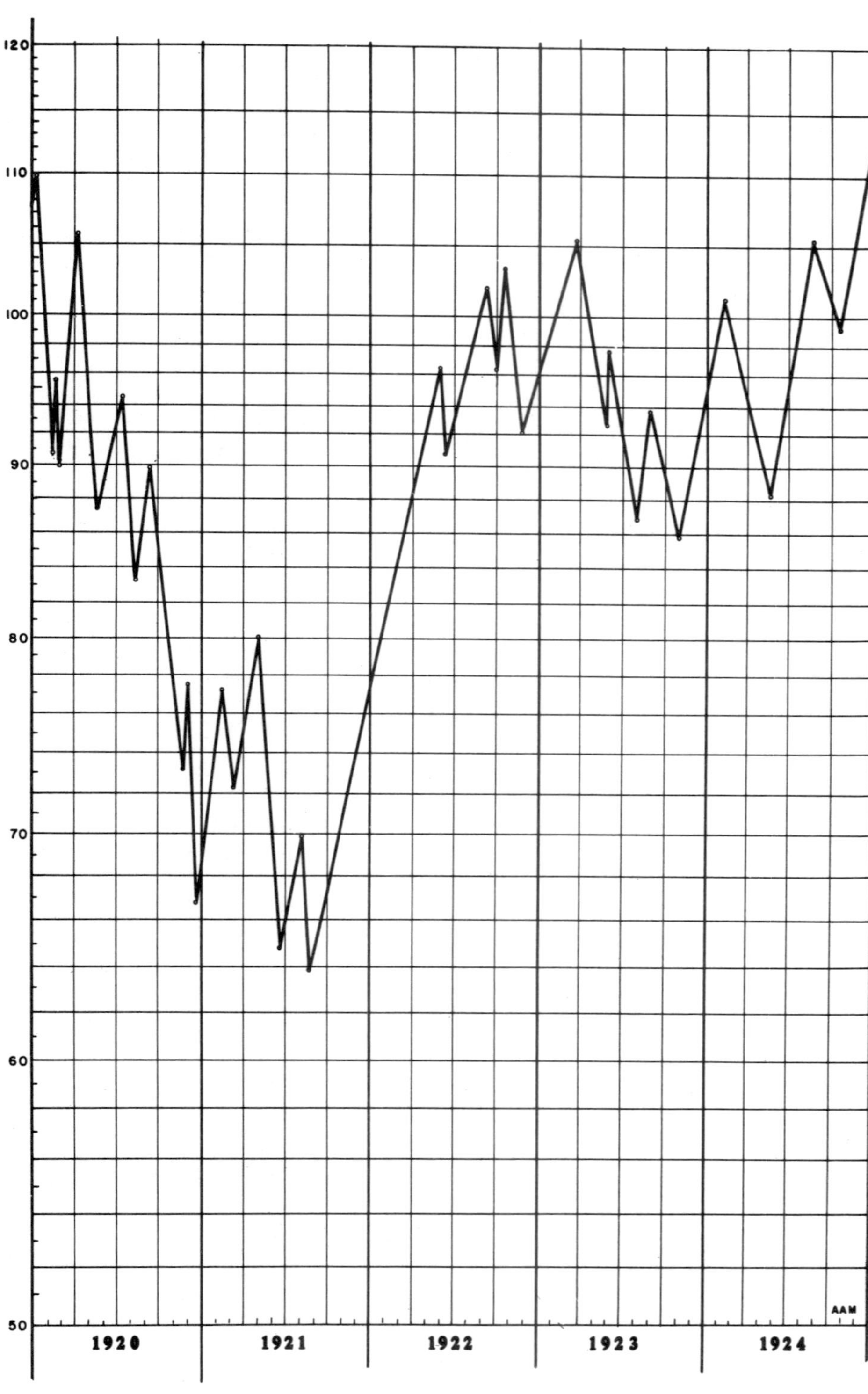

Appendix F
--Dow Jones Industrials, all swings over 5% --

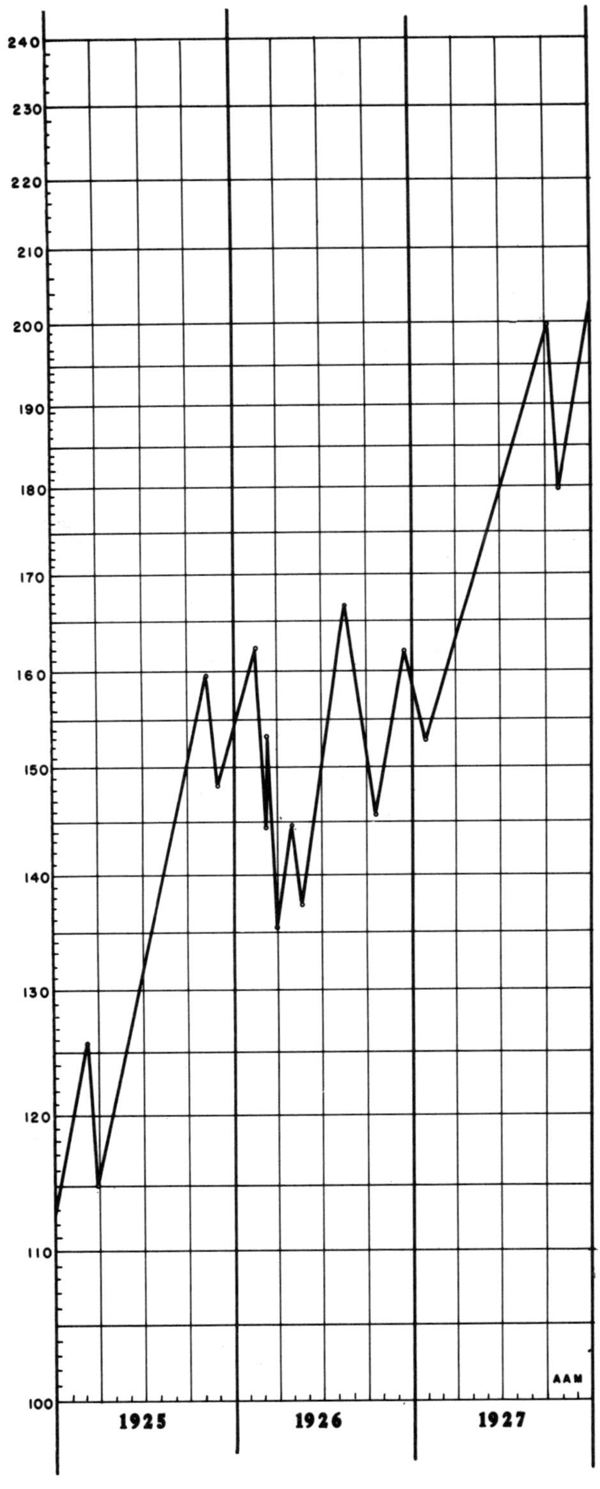

Appendix F

--Dow Jones Industrials, all swings over 5% --

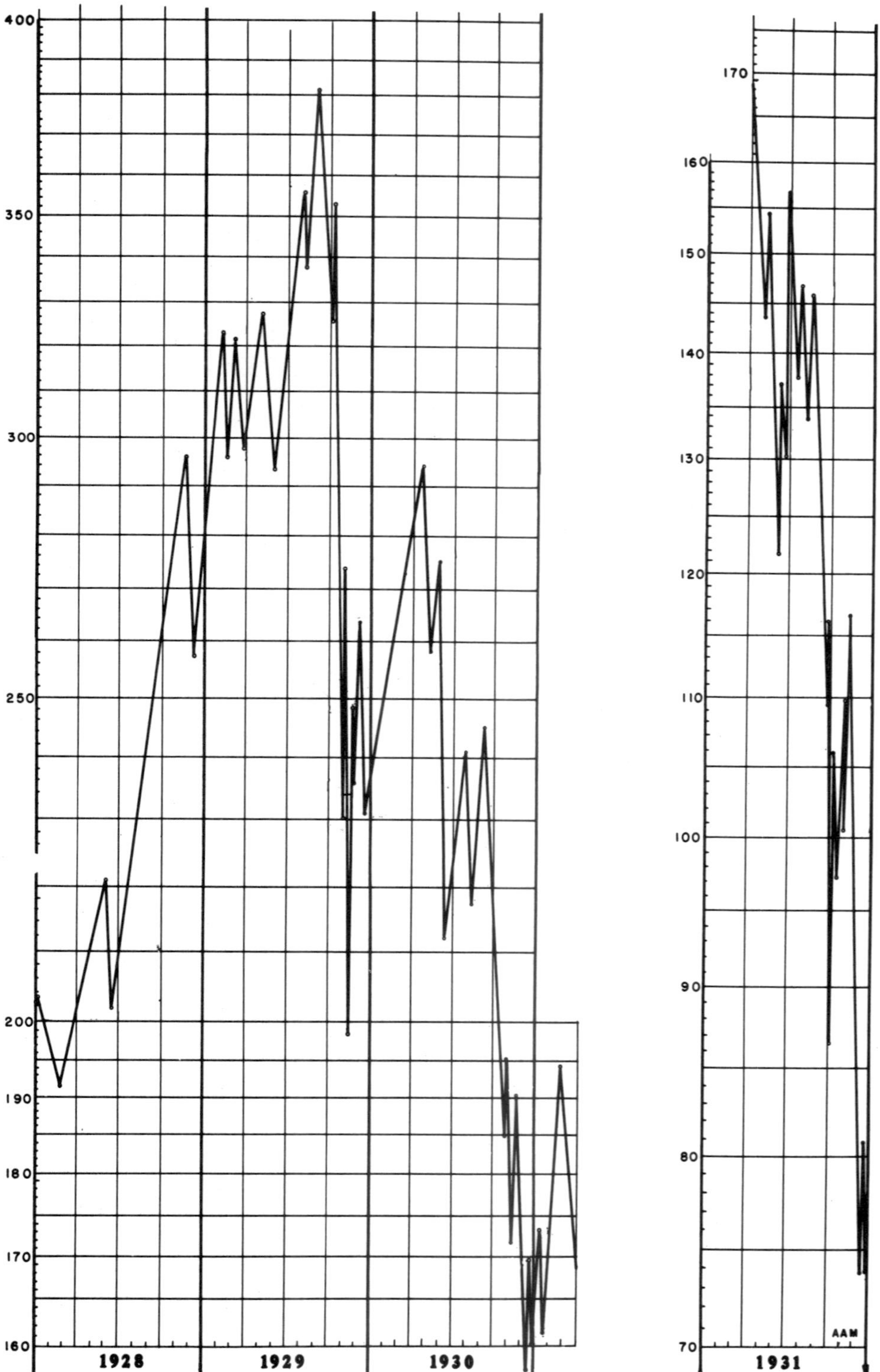

Appendix F
--Dow Jones Industrials, all swings over 5% --

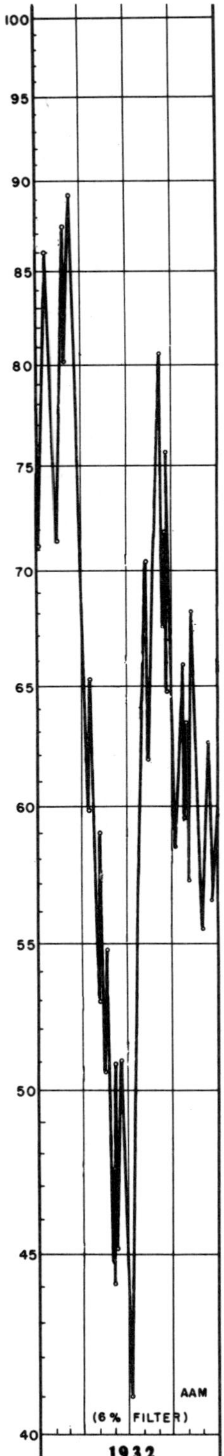

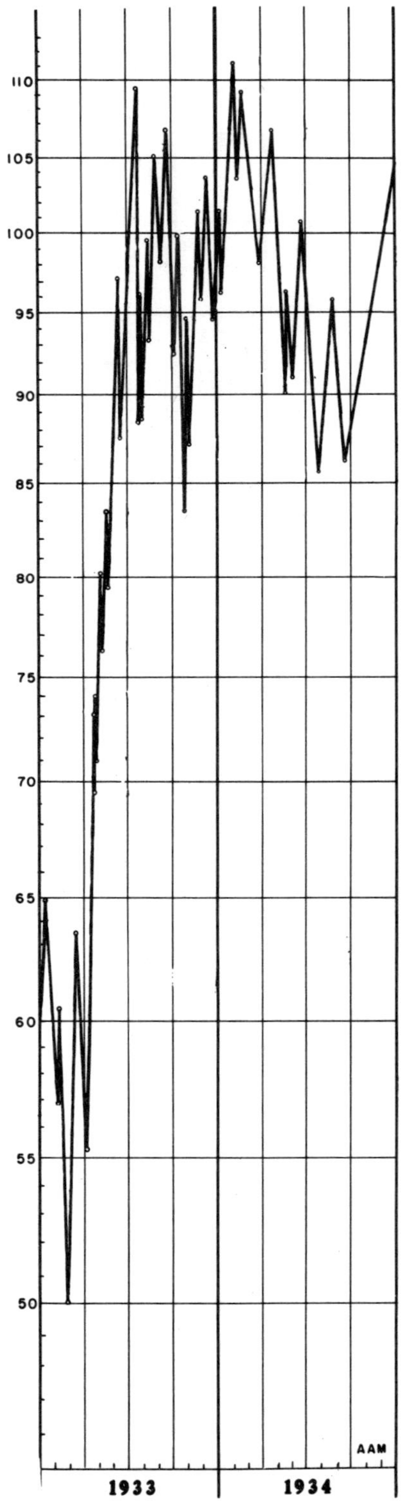

Appendix F
--Dow Jones Industrials, all swings over 5% --

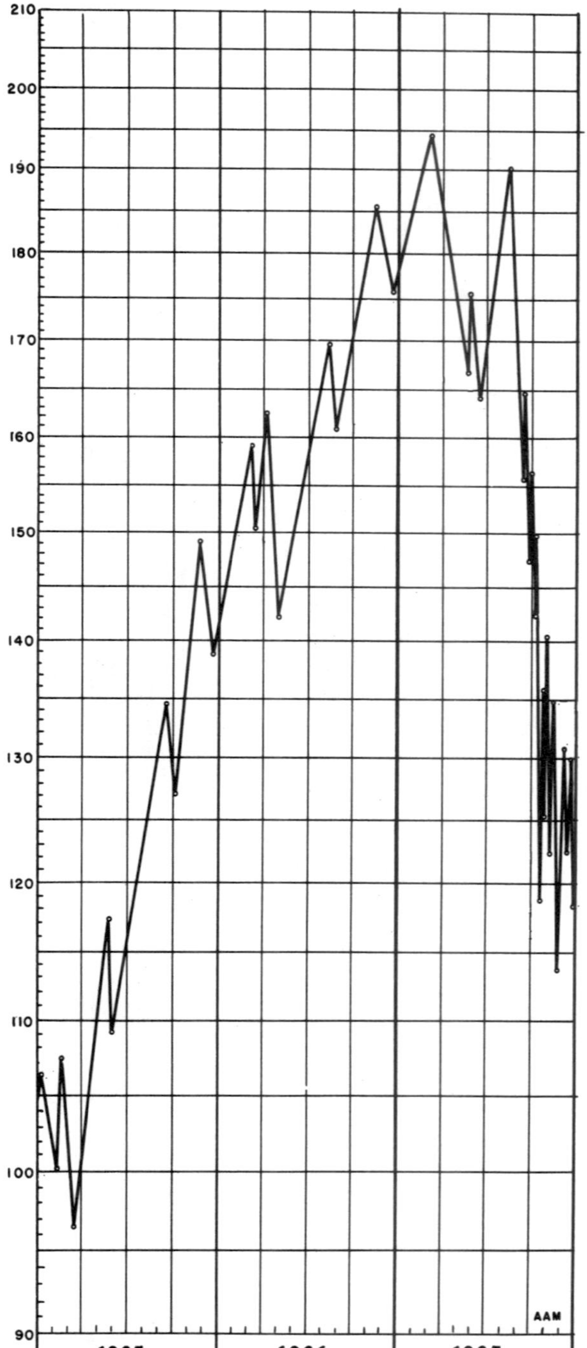

Appendix F
--Dow Jones Industrials, all swings over 5%

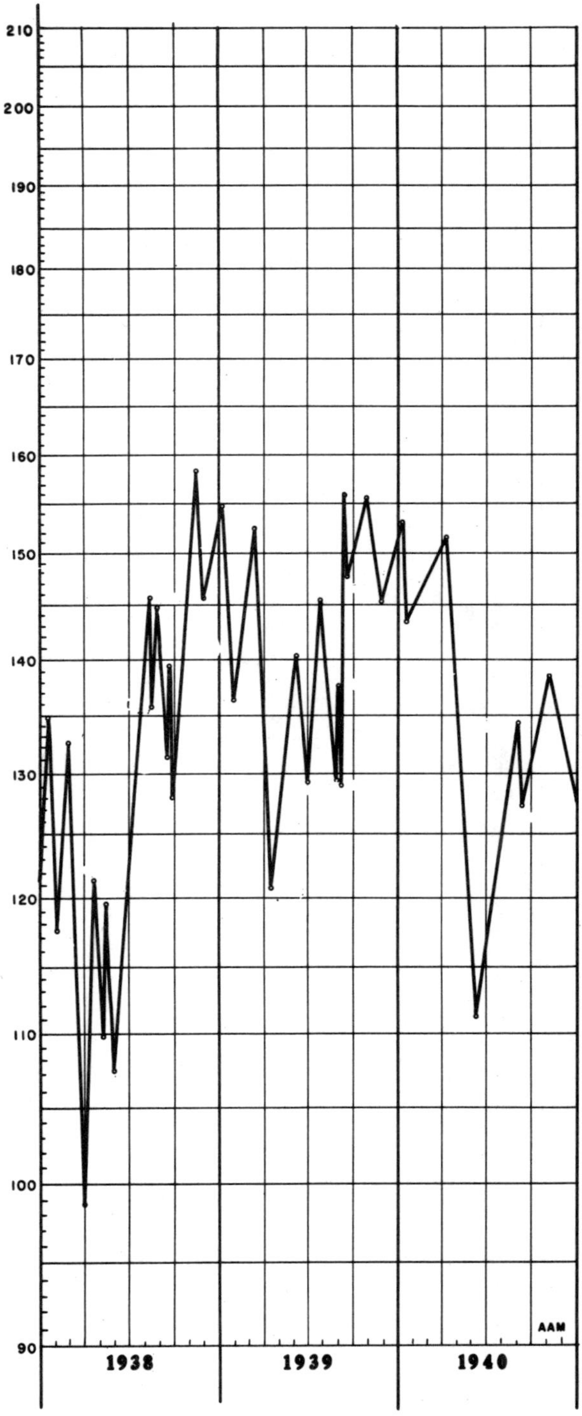

Appendix F

--Dow Jones Industrials, all swings over 5% --

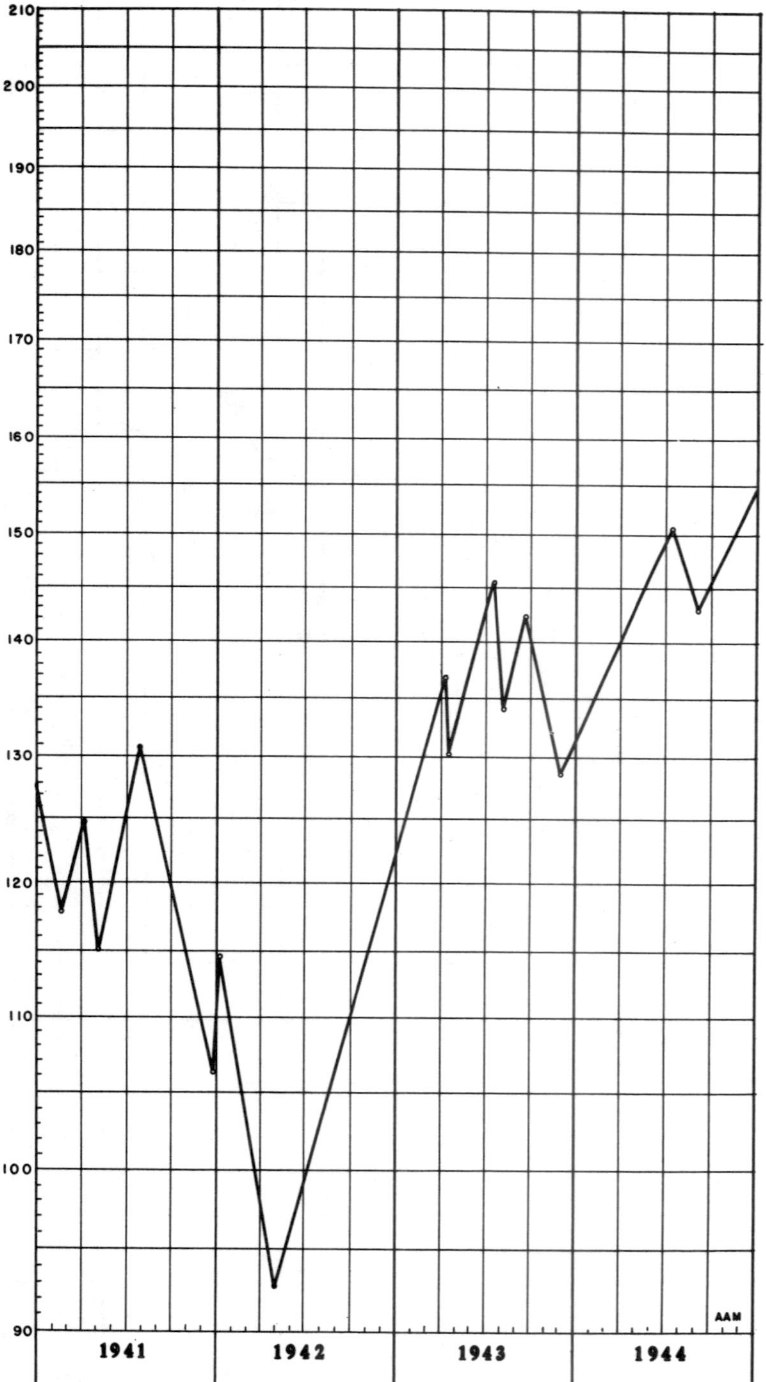

Appendix F
--Dow Jones Industrials, all swings over 5% --

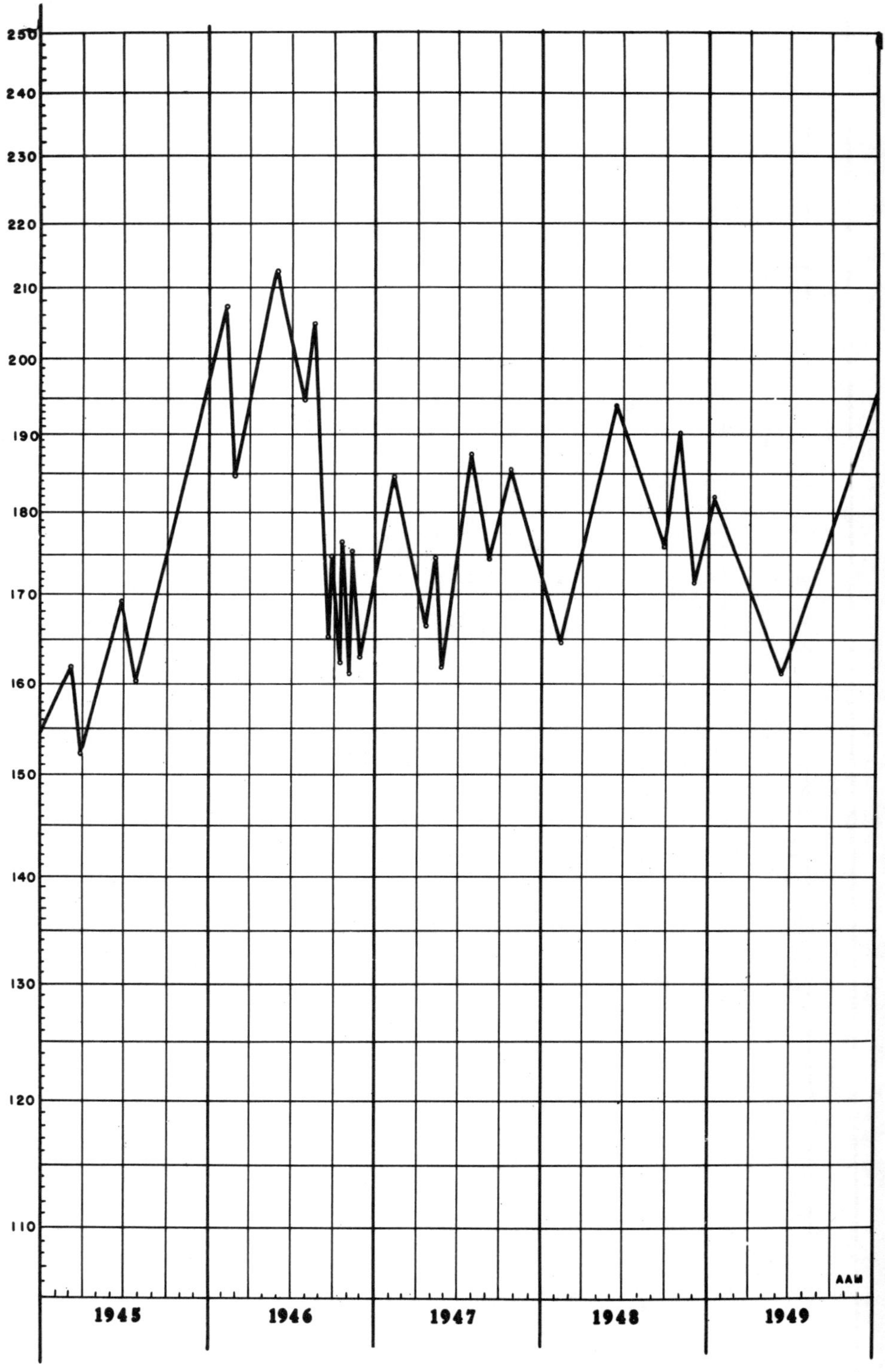

Appendix F
--Dow Jones Industrials, all swings over 5% --

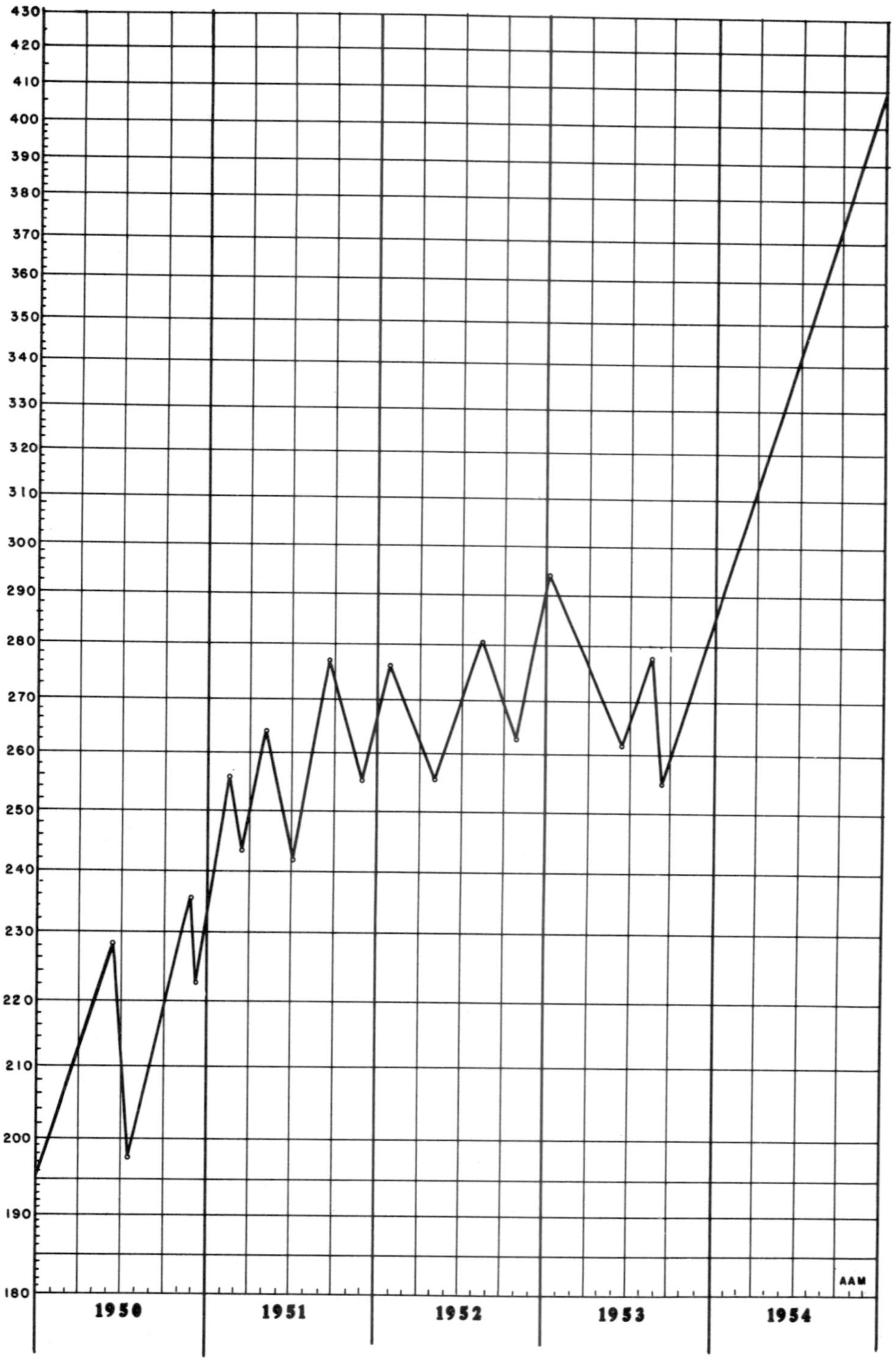

Appendix F

--Dow Jones Industrials, all swings over 5% --

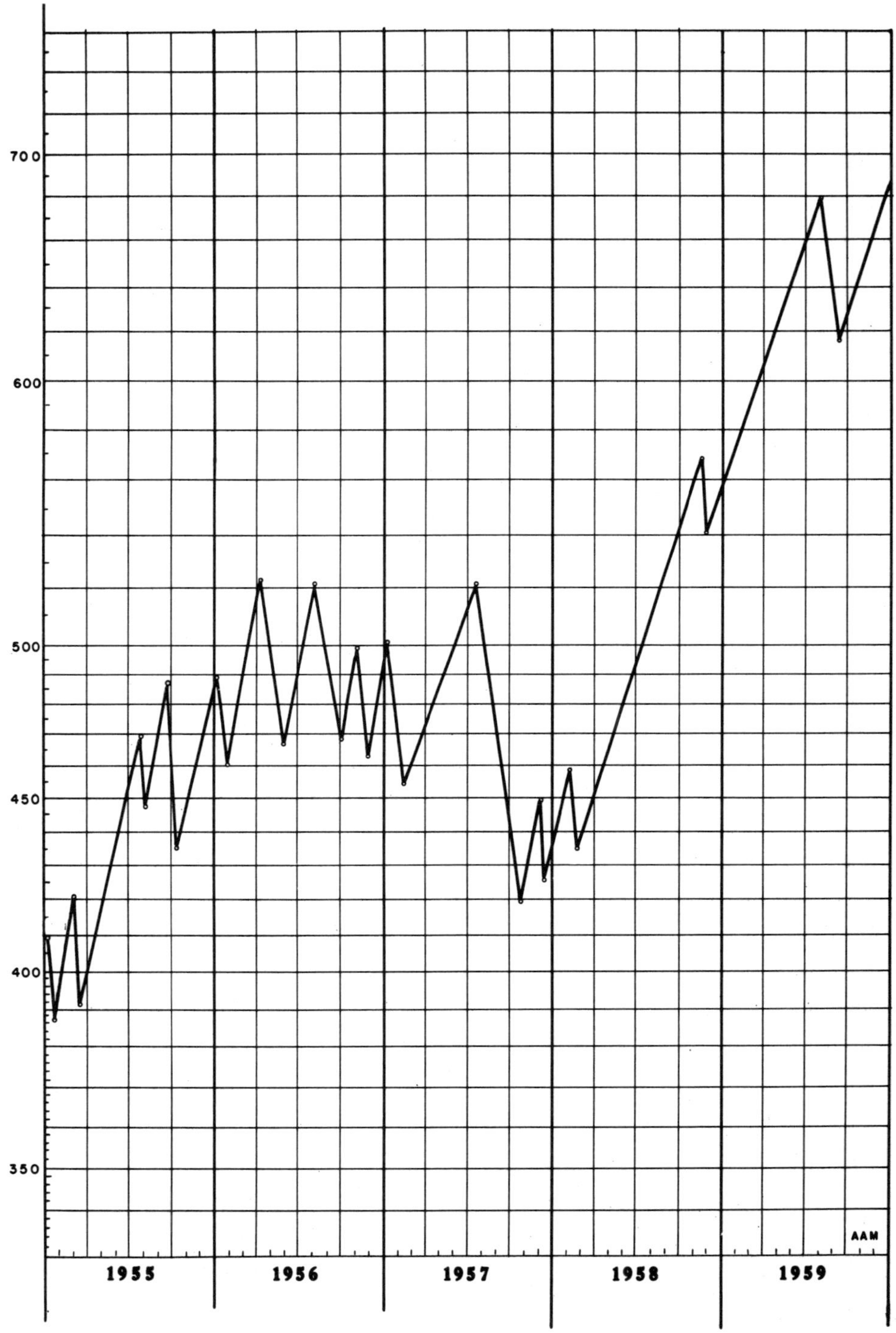

Appendix F
--Dow Jones Industrials, all swings over 5% --

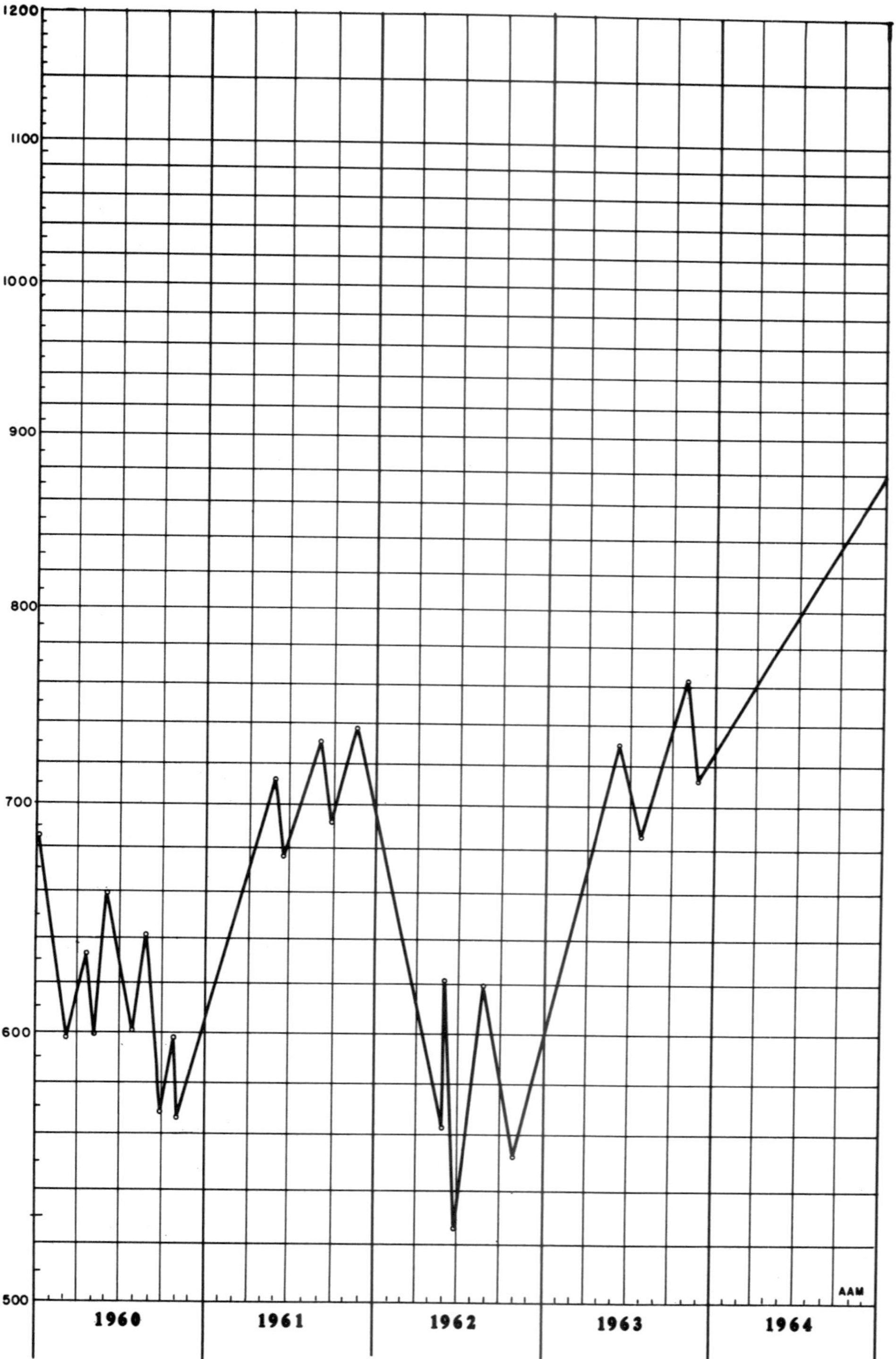

Appendix F
--Dow Jones Industrials, all swings over 5% --

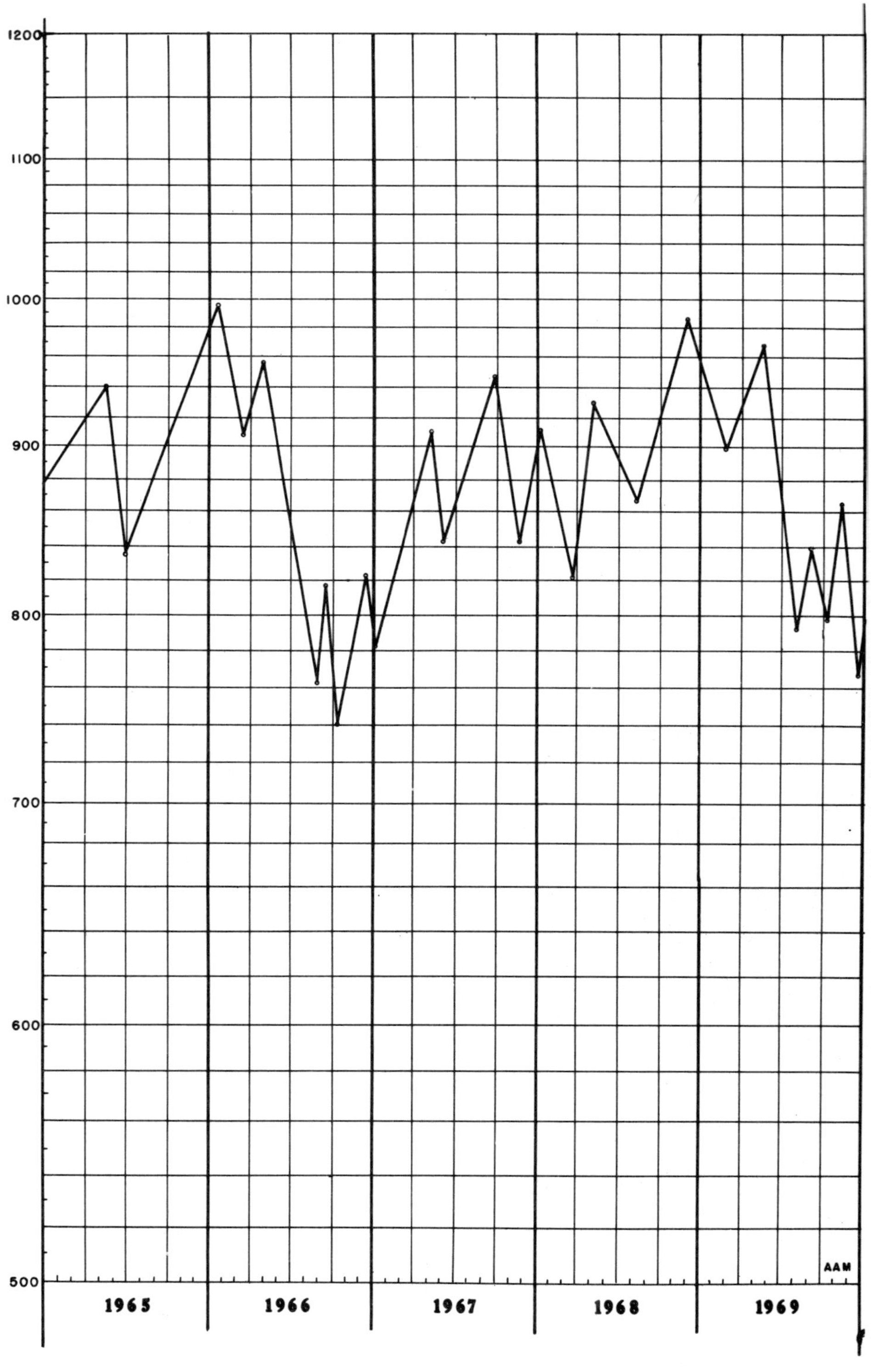

Appendix F
--Dow Jones Industrials, all swings over 5% --

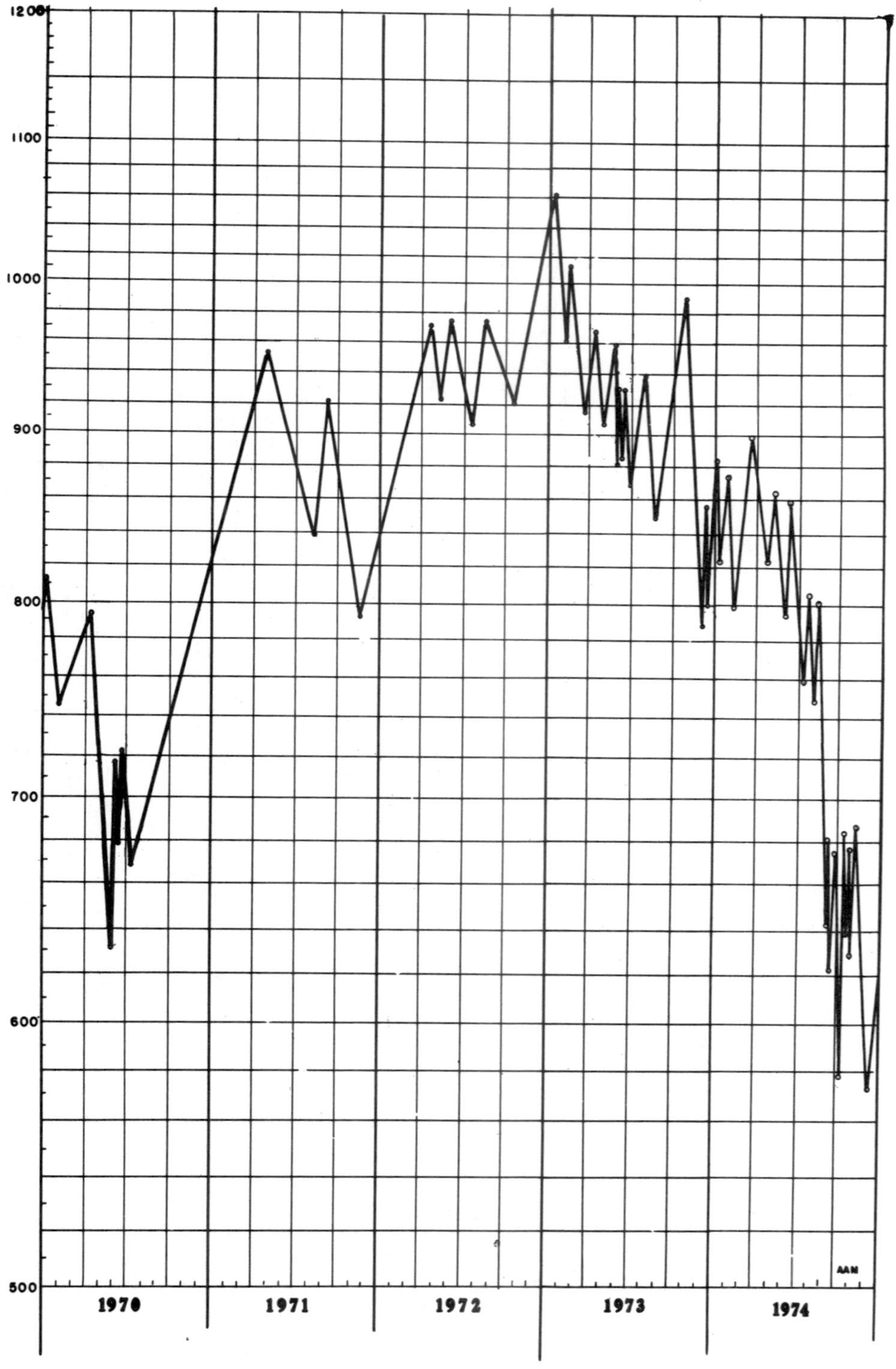

Appendix F
--Dow Jones Industrials, all swings over 5% --

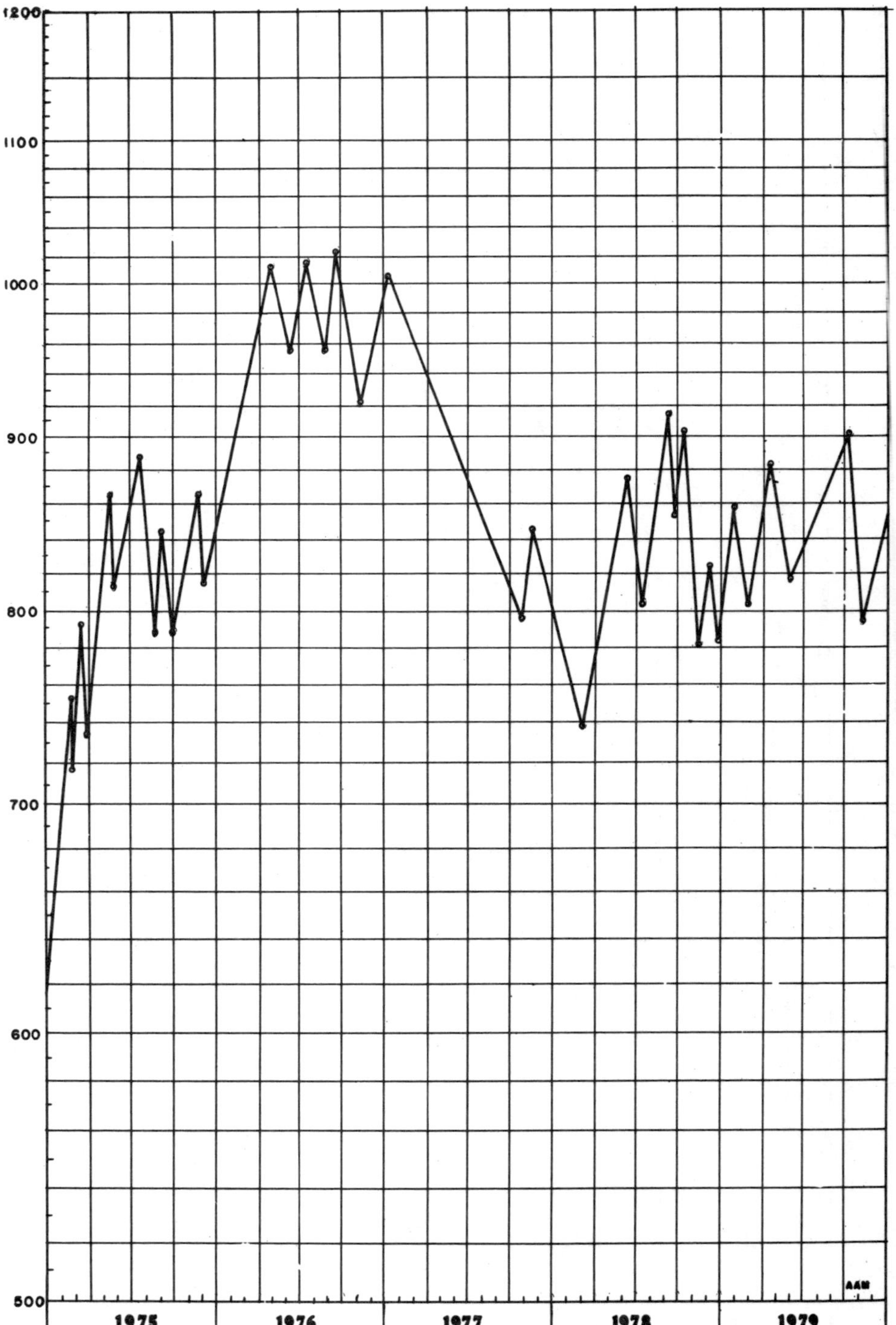

Appendix F
--Dow Jones Industrials, all swings over 5% --

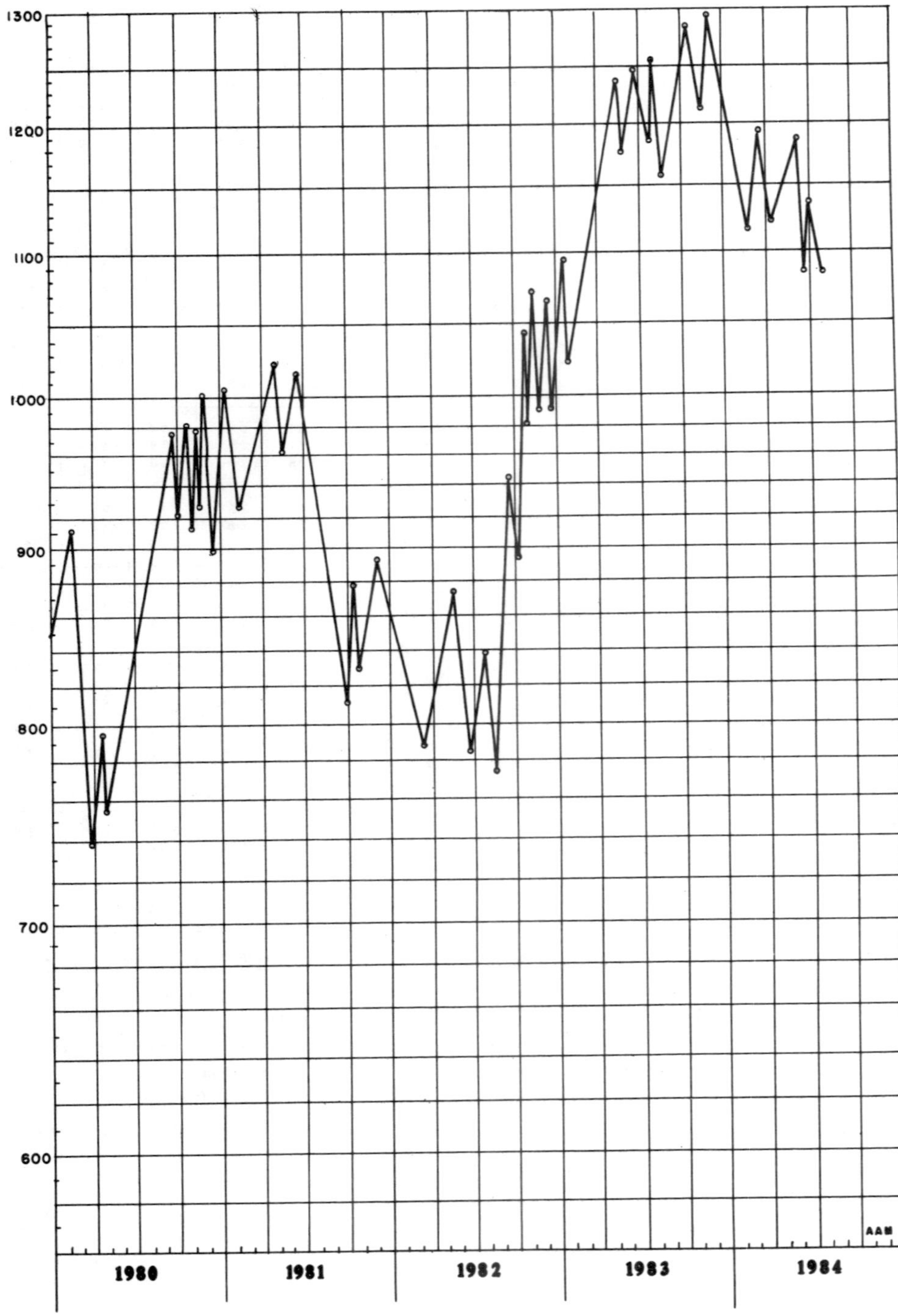

ELAPSED TIME CALCULATOR

DAY OF MONTH	DAY OF THE YEAR											
	MAR.	APR.	MAY	JUNE	JULY	AUG.	SEP.	OCT.	NOV.	DEC.	JAN.	FEB.
1	1	32	62	93	123	154	185	215	246	276	307	338
2	2	33	63	94	124	155	186	216	247	277	308	339
3	3	34	64	95	125	156	187	217	248	278	309	340
4	4	35	65	96	126	157	188	218	249	279	310	341
5	5	36	66	97	127	158	189	219	250	280	311	342
6	6	37	67	98	128	159	190	220	251	281	312	343
7	7	38	68	99	129	160	191	221	252	282	313	344
8	8	39	69	100	130	161	192	222	253	283	314	345
9	9	40	70	101	131	162	193	223	254	284	315	346
10	10	41	71	102	132	163	194	224	255	285	316	347
11	11	42	72	103	133	164	195	225	256	286	317	348
12	12	43	73	104	134	165	196	226	257	287	318	349
13	13	44	74	105	135	166	197	227	258	288	319	350
14	14	45	75	106	136	167	198	228	259	289	320	351
15	15	46	76	107	137	168	199	229	260	290	321	352
16	16	47	77	108	138	169	200	230	261	291	322	353
17	17	48	78	109	139	170	201	231	262	292	323	354
18	18	49	79	110	140	171	202	232	263	293	324	355
19	19	50	80	111	141	172	203	233	264	294	325	356
20	20	51	81	112	142	173	204	234	265	295	326	357
21	21	52	82	113	143	174	205	235	266	296	327	358
22	22	53	83	114	144	175	206	236	267	297	328	359
23	23	54	84	115	145	176	207	237	268	298	329	360
24	24	55	85	116	146	177	208	238	269	299	330	361
25	25	56	86	117	147	178	209	239	270	300	331	362
26	26	57	87	118	148	179	210	240	271	301	332	363
27	27	58	88	119	149	180	211	241	272	302	333	364
28	28	59	89	120	150	181	212	242	273	303	334	365
29	29	60	90	121	151	182	213	243	274	304	335	366
30	30	61	91	122	152	183	214	244	275	305	336	
31	31		92		153	184		245		306	337	

<u>To find number of days between two dates:</u>

(1) Put down 365. for each Feb.28 passed over.
(For a leap year Feb. 29 use 366.)

(2) Add "Day of the year" for the second date.

(3) Subtract "Day of the year" for the first date.

(4) Remainder is the number of days between the two dates.

<u>Example: April 24,1962 to March 12, 1964</u>

(1)	+ 365	(For Feb. 28, 1963)
	+ 366	(For Feb. 29, 1964)
(2)	+ 12	(For March 12, 1964)
	743	(Total)
(3)	− 55	(For April 24, 1962)
(4)	688	(Elapsed time in days)

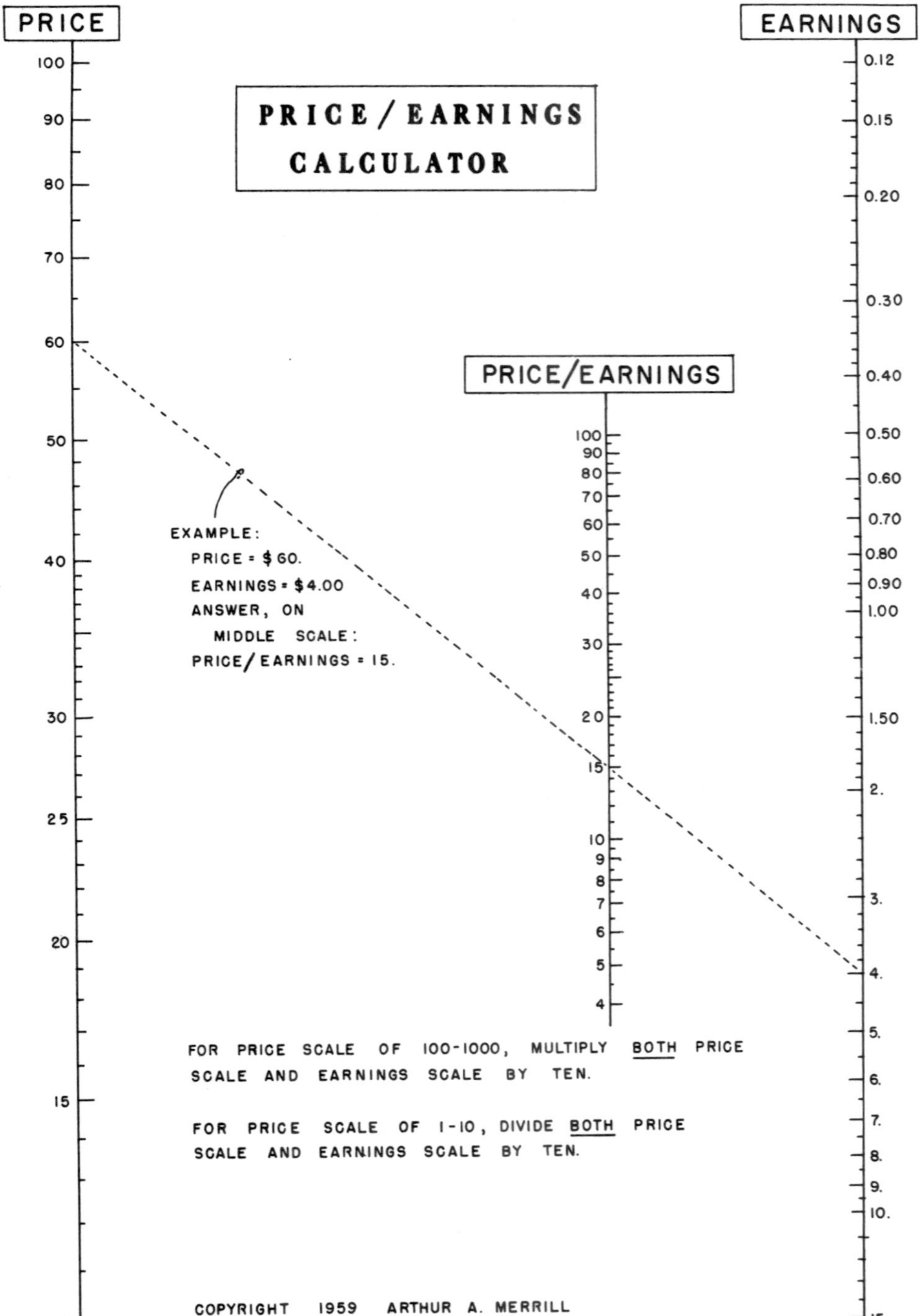
PRICE
EARNINGS
PRICE / EARNINGS CALCULATOR
PRICE/EARNINGS
100 90 80 70 60 50 40 30 25 20 15 10
0.12 0.15 0.20 0.30 0.40 0.50 0.60 0.70 0.80 0.90 1.00 1.50 2. 3. 4. 5. 6. 7. 8. 9. 10. 15.
100 90 80 70 60 50 40 30 20 15 10 9 8 7 6 5 4
EXAMPLE:
PRICE = $60.
EARNINGS = $4.00
ANSWER, ON MIDDLE SCALE:
PRICE/EARNINGS = 15.
FOR PRICE SCALE OF 100-1000, MULTIPLY BOTH PRICE SCALE AND EARNINGS SCALE BY TEN.
FOR PRICE SCALE OF 1-10, DIVIDE BOTH PRICE SCALE AND EARNINGS SCALE BY TEN.
COPYRIGHT 1959 ARTHUR A. MERRILL

-YEAR TYPE LETTER-

Go down column to first three digits of year then across to column of fourth digit, and obtain Year Type Letter.

	0	1	2	3	4	5	6	7	8	9
175	A	B		A	B	C	K	F	G	A
176	I	D	E	F	N	B	C	D	L	G
177	A	B	J	E	F	G	H	C	D	E
178	M	A	B	C	K	F	G	A	I	D
179	E	F	N	B	C	D	L	G	A	B
180	C	D	E	F	N	B	C	D	L	G
181	A	B	J	E	F	G	H	C	D	E
182	M	A	B	C	K	F	G	A	I	D
183	E	F	N	B	C	D	L	G	A	B
184	J	E	F	G	H	C	D	E	M	A
185	B	C	K	F	G	A	I	D	E	F
186	N	B	C	D	L	G	A	B	J	E
187	F	G	H	C	D	E	M	A	B	C
188	K	F	G	A	I	D	E	F	N	B
189	C	D	L	G	A	B	J	E	F	G
190	A	B	C	D	L	G	A	B	J	E
191	F	G	H	C	D	E	M	A	B	C
192	K	F	G	A	I	D	E	F	N	B
193	C	D	L	G	A	B	J	E	F	G
194	H	C	D	E	M	A	B	C	K	F
195	G	A	I	D	E	F	N	B	C	D
196	L	G	A	B	J	E	F	G	H	C
197	D	E	M	A	B	C	K	F	G	A
198	I	D	E	F	N	B	C	D	L	G
199	A	B	J	E	F	G	H	C	D	E
200	M	A	B	C	K	F	G	A	I	D
201	E	F	N	B	C	D	L	G	A	B
202	J	E	F	G	H	C	D	E	M	A
203	B	C	K	F	G	A	I	D	E	F
204	N	B	C	D	L	G	A	B	J	E
205	F	G	H	C	D	E	M	A	B	C

CALENDAR .... 1753 - 2059

TO USE: FIRST: OBTAIN YEAR TYPE LETTER FROM OPPOSITE PAGE,
THEN FIND MONTH,
GO STRAIGHT ACROSS TO YEAR TYPE LETTER,
THEN DOWN TO CALENDAR.

JAN. 31d.	E	L	G	N	D	K	A	H	C	J	B	I	F	M	31.d. JAN.
FEB. 28-29	B	I	D	K	A	H	E	L	G	N	F	M	C	J	28-29 FEB.
MAR. 31.d.	B	H	D	J	A	N	E	K	G	M	F	L	C	I	31.d. MAR.
APR. 30.d	F	L	A	N	E	K	B	H	D	J	C	I	G	M	30.d. APR.
MAY 31.d	D	J	F	L	C	I	G	M	B	H	A	N	E	K	31.d. MAY
JUNE 30d.	A	N	C	I	G	M	D	J	F	L	E	K	B	H	30.d. JUNE
JULY 31.d.	F	L	A	N	E	K	B	H	D	J	C	I	G	M	31.d. JULY
AUG. 31.d.	C	I	E	K	B	H	F	L	A	N	G	M	D	J	31.d. AUG.
SEP. 30.d.	G	M	B	H	F	L	C	I	E	K	D	J	A	N	30.d SEP.
OCT. 31.d.	E	K	G	M	D	J	A	N	C	I	B	H	F	L	31.d. OCT.
NOV. 30d.	B	H	D	J	A	N	E	K	G	M	F	L	C	I	30.d. NOV.
DEC. 31.d.	G	M	B	H	F	L	C	I	E	K	D	J	A	N	31.d. DEC.

S	M	Tu	W	Th	F	S
1	2	3	4	5	6	7
8	9	10	11	12	13	14
15	16	17	18	19	20	21
22	23	24	25	26	27	28
29	30	31				

S	M	Tu	W	Th	F	S
	1	2	3	4	5	6
7	8	9	10	11	12	13
14	15	16	17	18	19	20
21	22	23	24	25	26	27
28	29	30	31			

S	M	Tu	W	Th	F	S
		1	2	3	4	5
6	7	8	9	10	11	12
13	14	15	16	17	18	19
20	21	22	23	24	25	26
27	28	29	30	31		

S	M	Tu	W	Th	F	S
					1	2
3	4	5	6	7	8	9
10	11	12	13	14	15	16
17	18	19	20	21	22	23
24	25	26	27	28	29	30
31						

S	M	Tu	W	Th	F	S
			1	2	3	4
5	6	7	8	9	10	11
12	13	14	15	16	17	18
19	20	21	22	23	24	25
26	27	28	29	30	31	

S	M	Tu	W	Th	F	S
						1
2	3	4	5	6	7	8
9	10	11	12	13	14	15
16	17	18	19	20	21	22
23	24	25	26	27	28	29
30	31					

EXAMPLE:
JULY 4, 1776
YEAR TYPE: H
DAY OF WEEK: THURSDAY

S	M	Tu	W	Th	F	S
				1	2	3
4	5	6	7	8	9	10
11	12	13	14	15	16	17
18	19	20	21	22	23	24
25	26	27	28	29	30	31

Appendix J.

Bibliography; Investment:

Allen, Leon B.: Method for Stock Profits; Doubleday 1962
Appel, Gerald: Selected Readings in the Stock Market; Systems and Forecasts 1974
Appel,Gerald:Stock Market Trading Systems;Dow Jones 1980
Ayres, Leonard P. : Turning Points in Business Cycles;Macmillan 1940
Barnes, Dr.Leo: Your Investments; Am.Res.Council, annual
Barron's: National Business and Financial Weekly
Baruch,Bernard M.:My Own Story; Holt 1957
Bean,L.H.:How to Predict the Stock Market:Luce 1962
Bernhard, A.:Evaluation of Common Stocks:Simon and Schuster 1959
Black,Hillel:Watchdogs of Wall Street:Morrow 1962
Bolton, A.Hamilton:The Elliott Wave Principle 1960
Bratt,Dr.Elmer Clark:Business Cycles and Forecasting:Irwin 1937
Bretz,William G.:Juncture Recognition;Vantage 1972
Brooks,John:The Seven Fat Years;Harper 1954
Burns and Mitchell:Measuring Business Cycles;NBEC 1946
Butler,Kavesh,Platt:Methods and Techniques of Business Forecasting;Prentice Hall 1974
Campbell, Don G.:Let's Take Stock;Bobbs Merrill 1939
Carpenter,H.G.:A Successful Investor's Letters to His Son;Simon and Schuster 1934
Carpenter,H.G.:This is Investment Management;Scarborough 1946
Cary,Elgin:Profitable Spreading Strategies;Austin 1976
Chestnut, George A.Jr.:Stock Market Analysis;Am.Investors 1964
Clasing,Henry K.Jr.:Dow Jones Irwin Guide to Put and Call Options;Dow Jones Irwin 1975
Cobleigh,Dr.I.:How to Get Rich Buying Stocks;David McKay 1959
Cobleigh and Dorfman:Dowbeaters;Macmillan 1979
Cogan, L.Peter:Rhythmic Cycles of Optimism and Pessimism; William Frederick 1969
Cohen,Zinburg,Zeikel:Guide to Intelligent Investing;Dow Jones Irwin 1977
Cootner,P.H.:Random Character of Stock Market Prices, MIT 1964
Costa and Jacwin, How to Accumulate Wealth through Stock Speculation.;Kent 1958
Cragg,Alliston:Understanding the Stock Market;Garden City 1929
Crane,Burton:The Sophisticated Investor;Simon and Schuster. 1959
Dahl,Curtiss:Consistent Profits in the Stock Market;TriState 1951

deVilliers,Victor:Point and Figure Method;Stock Market Pub.1933
Dewey and Dakin:The Science of Prediction;Henry Holt 1947
Dines,James:Technical Analysis Made Easy;1967
Dines,James:The Invisible Crash;Random House 1975
Drew,G.:New Methods for Profit in the Stock Market;Metcalf 1941
Ellinger,A.G.:The Art of Investment;Bowes 1971
Elliott,R.N.:The Wave Principle;1938
Elliott,R.N.:Articles in Financial World August 1939
Elliott,R.N.:Nature's Law;1946
Engel,Louis:How to Buy Stocks;Bantam 1953
Epstein,Dr.R.C.:Making Money in Today's Market;Economica 1959
Farrell,Maurice L.:Dow Jones Investors' Handbook;Dow Jones 1954
Farrell,M.L.(Ed) Dow Jones Averages 1885-1970;Dow Jones 1972
Felsen,Jerry:Cybernetic Approach to Stock Market Analysis;Exposition 1975
Filer,Herbert:Understanding Put and Call Options;Crown 1959
Fisher,Philip A.:Paths to Wealth through Common Stocks; Prentice Hall 1960
Fisher,Philip A.:Common Stocks and Uncommon Profits;Harper 1958
Fosback,Norman G.:Stock Market Logic;Inst.for Econ.Res.1976
Gaylord,Sherwood:Sensible Speculation with Put and Call Options;Simon and Schuster 1976
Gingold,O.J.:Making and Keeping Stock Market Profits; Barron's 1937
Gordon,William:Stock Market Indicators:Investors Press 1968
Granville,Joseph E.:A Strategy of Daily Stock Market Timing;Prentice Hall 1960
Granville,Joseph E.:New Strategy of Daily Stock Market Timing;Prentice Hall 1976
Gutman,Walter K.:You Only Have to Get Rich Once;Dutton 1961
Haller,Gilbert:The Haller Theory of Stock Market Trends; Haller 1965
Hamilton, William Peter:The Stock Market Barometer;Russell 1922
Harahus,David:On Market Speculation;Harahus 1977
Hardy,C.O.:Odd Lot Trading;Brookings Institution
Heiby,Walter A.:The New Dynamic Synthesis:Inst.of Dyn.Syn.1967
Heiby,Walter A.:Stock Market Profits through Dynamic Synthesis:Inst.of Dyn.Syn.1965
Hriston,Loucas P.:Professional Approach to Investment Profits:Larchmont 1960
Hurst,J.M.:Profit Magic of Stock Market Timing;Prentice Hall 1970
Investor's Intelligence:Encyclopedia of Stock Market Techniques;inv.Intell.
Jiler,William L.:How Charts Can Help You in the Stock Market;Comm.Res.1962

Katz,Howard:The Short Term;1964
Kelly,Fred C.:Why You Win or Lose;Kelly 1930
Kelly,Fred C.:Psychology of Speculation;Fraser 1930
Krow,Harvey A.:Stock Market Behavior;Random House 1969
Lefevre,Edwin:Reminiscences of a Stock Market Operator; Pocket Books 1923
Leffler,George L.:The Stock Market;Ronald 1951
Lempenar,J.A.:How to Take a Fortune Out of Wall Street; Income Builder 1955
Levien,J.R.:Anatomy of a Crash;Traders Press 1966
Levy,Robert:Relative Strength Concept;Inv.Int. 1968
Levy,Robert: Article,Journal of Commerce of U.of Chicago, July 1971
Levy,S.J. and David:Profits;Harper and Row
Lewinsohn,Richard:Science,Prophesy and Prediction;Bell 1961
Lloyd,Humphrey:The Moving Balance System;Windsor 1976
Loeb,G.M.:Battle For Investment Survival;Simon and Schuster 1935
Lohman,Philipp H.:Art of Investing;Hawthorn 1972
Magee,John:General Semantics of Wall Street;Magee 1958
Magee and Edwards:Technical Analysis of Stock Trends;Magee 1948
Maginn and Tuttle (ed,):Managing Investment Portfolios; Warren Gorham Lamont 1983
Mahoney,John E.:Buy Low Sell High;Pagorian 1978
Malkiel,Burton G.:A Random Walk down Wall Street;Norton 1973
Mamis,Justin and Robert:When to Sell;Farrar Straus 1977
Mayer,Martin:Wall Street Men and Money;Harper and Bro.1955
Mennis,Edmund A.:Investment Trusts;Am.Inst.for Econ.Res.1937
Merrill,Arthur A.:Behavior of Prices on Wall Street First Edition;Analysis 1966
Merrill,Arthur A.:Filtered Waves Basic Theory;Analysis 1977
Merrill,Arthur A.:Bias in Daily and Weekly Wave Patterns; Analysis 1980
Merrill Arthur A.:M.and W.Wave Patterns;Analysis 1983
Merrill,Arthur C.:Investing in the Scientific Revolution; Doubleday 1962
Miller,Lowell:The Perfect Investment;Dutton 1983
Mills,Frederick C.:Price Quantity Interactions in Business Cycles;NBER 1946
Moore,Geoffrey H.:Business Cycle Indicators;Princeton 1961
Neill,Humphrey B.:It Pays to be Contrary;Fraser 1962
Neill,Humphrey B.:Tape Reading and Market Tactics;Forbes 1931
Nelson,S.A.:ABC of Wall Street,Nelson 1904 reprint Fraser.
N.Y.Stock Exchange:Securities and Investing; 1965
Notley,I.S.:Trend and Cycle Analysis:Dominion 1977
O'Connor,William:Stocks,Wheat and Pharaohs;Wener 1961
Palmer,John R.:How to Buy Stocks;Bantam 1967

Peisner,Robert N.:How to Select Rapid Growth Stocks;Dutton 1966
Prechter,Robert (ed.):Major Works of R.N.Elliott;New Classics 1980
Prechter and Frost:Elliott Wave Principle;New Classics 1978
Preston,Charles:World of the Wall Street Journal;Simon and Schuster 1959
Pring,Martin:Technical Analysis Explained;McGraw Hill 1980
Rhea,Robert:The Dow Theory;Daniel Smith 1932
Rhea,Robert:Dow's Theory;Simon and Schuster 1938
Russell,Richard:Dow Theory Today;Fraser 1958
Sergeant,William P.:Stock Market Behavior;Exposition 1957
Schabacker,R.W.:Stock Market Theory and Practice;Forbes 1930
Schaefer,E.George:How I Helped More Than 10,000 Investors;Prentice Hall 1960
Schwed,Fred Jr.:Where are the Customers' Yachts?; Simon and Schuster 1940
Sharpe,William:Investments;Prentice Hall 1978
Shirk,Gertrude: Articles in "Cycles", the Journal of the Foundation for the Study of Cycles, Pittsburgh
Shulsky,Sam:Stock Buying Guide;Arco 1959
Shumate and Fritz:Making the Dow Theory Work;Russell 1960
Shultz,H.D.:Bear Markets;Prentice Hall 1964
Smith,Clifford W.Jr.:Option Pricing;U.of Rochester 1975
Stabler,C.Norman:How to Read the Financial News;Harper 1932
Stansbury,Charles B.:The Dow Theory Explained;Russell 1938
Stearns,Linhart:How to Live With Your Investments;Simon and Schuster 1955
Sterling,Dorothy:Wall Street;Doubleday 1955
Taylor,Owen:Stop Orders;Stock Market Pub.1932
Valentine and Mennis:Quantitative Techniques for Financial Analysis;Irwin 1980
Watts,Dickson G.:Speculation as a Fine Art;Traders Press 1965
Wheelan,Alexander:Study Helps in Point and Figure; Andrews Technical Studies
Williams,LarryR.:Secret of Selecting Stocks;Conceptual 1972
Williams and Noseworthy:Sure Thing Commodity Trading; Windsor 1977
Wilson,Louise L.Catalogue of Cycles;Foundation for the Study of Cycles 1964
Wise,T.A.:The Insiders;Lehman 1957
Wright,Wilson:Forecasting for Profit;Wiley 1947
Wyckoff,Richard D.:Studies in Tape Reading; Traders Press 1910
Wyckoff,Richard D.:Trading and Investing;Wyckoff 1931
Wyckoff,R.D.:Wall Street Ventures and Adventures;Harper 1930
Zahorchak,Michael G.:Art of Low Risk Investing;Van Nostrand 1972
Zahorchak,Michael D.:Favorable Executions;Van Nostrand 1974
Zahorchak,Michael D.(ed.):Wheeler Papers,Climate;Tide

Appendix K.

Bibliography; Statistics:

Arkin and Colton:Tables for Statisticians;Barnes and Noble 1950
Arkin and Colton:Statistical Methods;Barnes and Noble 1934
Burington and May:Handbook of Probability and Statistics; McGraw Hill 1970
Byrkit,Donald:Elements of Statistics;Van Nostrand 1972
Chou,Ya-Lun:Statistical Analysis;Holt Rinehart 1969
Croxton and Cowden:Applied General Statistics;Prentice Hall 1939
Dixon and Massey:Introduction to Statistical Analysis; McGraw Hill 1951
Dodes,Irving A.:Introduction to Statistical Analysis;Hayden 1974
Downie and Heath:Basic Statistical Methods;Harper and Row 1959
Ezekiel,Mordecai:Methods of Correlation Analysis;Wiley 1930
Franzblau,Abraham:A Primer of Statistics for Non-Statisticians;Harcourt Brace 1958
Hayslett,H.T.Jr.:Statistics Made Simple;Doubleday 1968
Hoel,Paul:Elementary Statistics;Wiley 1960
Hogben,Lancelot:Mathematics for the Million;Norton 1937
Hultquist,Robert:Introduction to Statistics;Holt Rinehart 1969
Kazmier,Leonard:Business Statistics;McGraw Hill 1976
Kendall,Maurice:Time Series;Hafner 1973
Kimball,Gregory:How to Use and Misuse Statistics;Prentice Hall 1978
King and Julstrom:Applied Statistics Using the Computer; Alfred 1982
Korin,Basil P.:Introduction to Statistical Methods;Winthrop 1977
Langley,Russell:Practical Statistics;Dover 1968
Lentner,Marvin:Elementary Applied Statistics;Bogden Quigley 1972
Moroney,M.J.:Facts from Figures;Pelican 1951
Mosteller,Rourke,Thomas:Probability and Statistics; Addison Wesley 1961
Naiman,Rosenfeld,Zirkel:Understanding Statistics;McGraw Hill 1977
Neiswanger,W.A.:Elementary Statistical Methods;Macmillan 1966
Nemenyi,Dixon,White,Hedstrom:Statistics from Scratch; Holden Day 1977

Neville and Kennedy;Basic Statistical Methods;International 1964
Neyman,J.:First Course in Probability and Statistics;Holt Rinehart 1950
Nielsen,Kaj L.:Methods in Numerical Analysis;Macmillan 1956
Noether,Gottfried:Guide to Probability and Statistics; Addison Wesley 1961
O'Donovan,Thomas:Short Term Forecasting;Wiley 1983
Parzen,Emanuel(ed.):Time Series Analysis Papers;Holden Day 1967
Reichard,Robert S.:The Numbers Game;McGraw Hill 1972
Rowntree,Derek:Statistics Without Tears;Scribners 1981
Sanders,Murph,Eng:Statistics;McGraw Hill 1976
Shewhart and Deming:Statistical Method;Dept.Agriculture 1939
Siegel,Sidney:Nonparametric Statistics;McGraw Hill 1956
Smith, John H.:Tests of Significance;U.of Chicago 1939
Snedecor,George W.:Statistical Methods;Collegiate 1937
Spiegel,Murray R.:Statistics;McGraw Hill 1961
Summers and Peters:Basic Statistics in Business;Wadsworth 1973
Wallis and Roberts:Statistics;Free Press 1956

About the author:

Arthur A.Merrill, BS, MBA, devoted 33 years to the General Electric Company, in engineering, statistics, planning, forecasting, and management. Since 1962 he has been President of Merrill Analysis Inc., and has edited a statistical letter "Technical Trends", to help investors in their decisions. He is a Past International President of SPEBSQSA, Secretary of the Society for the Investigation of Recurring Events, a member of the Foundation for the Study of Cycles, Mensa, Intertel, the Market Technicians Association, the New York Society of Security Analysts, and a Fellow in the Financial Federation. He is the recipient of the the Fourth Annual Award of the Market Technicians Association. His home is in Chappaqua, New York.